"Moses stretched out his hand over the sea; and the Lord caused the sea to go back by a strong east wind . . . and the waters were divided." (Ex. 14:21.)

The power of faith. Is it present in your life? Or does it lie dormant, amounting to little more than a wavering positive attitude in time of need?

In *Living by the Power of Faith,* Elder Gene R. Cook shares insights on how to obtain, increase, and exercise faith to make your life richer and more productive. What can you expect after learning how to draw on the power of faith? "You can expect God to keep his promises and to bring to pass his will," says Elder Cook. "He will fulfill all his words, and he will grant you your righteous desires according to your faith."

Elder Gene R. Cook is a member of the First Quorum of the Seventy in The Church of Jesus Christ of Latter-day Saints.

Donna —

this book has helped me better understand the power and the gift we have in our faith.

Living
by the
Power
of **Faith**

Hope it is en-joyable and in-spiring to you too. ♡ Gwenne

Living
by the
Power
of Faith

Gene R. Cook

Deseret Book

Salt Lake City, Utah

Deseret Book is a registered trademark of Deseret Book Company.

First printing in paperbound edition, March 1991

ISBN 0-87579-526-9

Printed in the United States of America
10   9   8   7   6   5   4   3

To my wife and family,
who have been instrumental
in helping me
to better live by faith.

Contents

Contents

Acknowledgments

May my parents, brothers, sister, and grandparents know of my indebtedness to them for teaching me of the Lord and of the true pathway to eternal life. May my wife and children know of my indebtedness to them for providing life's experiences in which to exercise faith.

I would like to thank particularly Kristine Buchanan, my devoted secretary, who did much of the typing and editing of the materials that were used in this book, and Karen Pratt, who assisted in the original editing of some of the material in its early stages. Thanks also goes to Jack M. Lyon, associate editor at Deseret Book Company, who edited the manuscript and greatly assisted in its compilation.

I would especially like to thank the Lord and his many children throughout the world who have been such an inspiration to me as examples of how to live by faith.

I would like to make it clear that I alone am responsible for any errors in this book. The book is not in any way an official publication of The Church of Jesus Christ of Latter-day Saints, and the ideas in it do not necessarily represent the views of the Church or of Deseret Book Company.

Chapter One

The Power of Faith

On July 29, 1977, Sister Cook and I had just finished visiting the Bolivia Santa Cruz Mission and were stalled in the Cochabamba, Bolivia, airport for some five hours. I recall that we were very tired, having had few hours of sleep the night before. We were both delighted to have a few hours of rest in the airport. As I was drifting off to sleep, I had a very strong feeling that I should awaken and write down some ideas. The desire to sleep was strong, but the promptings of the Spirit were more powerful. I did write; in fact, I wrote for nearly three hours, solving some organizational problems I had struggled with for a number of years previously. I felt a great outpouring of the Spirit on that day and excitedly wrote down each inspired thought. The experience took most of the time of the delay.

We were then off to La Paz, Bolivia. We were graciously met by President and Sister Chase Allred at the airport and driven in their van to the mission office. We left our luggage and briefcase in the locked van.

Upon entering the office, the president was confronted with the difficult case of a woman whose husband was dying. While President Allred and I assisted with her needs, Sisters Cook and Allred left in a car for the mission home.

When the president and I returned to the van, I realized immediately that all of our goods were gone but assumed that Sister Cook had taken them with her to the mission home. While we were driving toward the home, I discovered that the right front wind wing had been damaged and began to fear that our goods had been stolen.

Arriving at the mission home, we found that our luggage had indeed been stolen. The loss of a substantial amount of money and all our clothing created an immediate but only temporary problem. More disheartening was the fact that my scriptures were in my briefcase along with the inspired ideas I had just received in Cochabamba. The overwhelming sensation of discouragement, anger, and inability to do anything about the situation was overpowering.

My wife and I prayed alone. We prayed with those present. We tried to enjoy our dinner but could not. Who could know of the great loss I personally felt? The scriptures had been given to me as a young man by my parents, a sacred inscription placed in one of them by my mother and in the other by my since-deceased father. I had spent literally thousands of hours marking and cross-referencing (and loving every moment of it) in the only tangible earthly possessions I had ever considered of much value. I had on many occasions instructed my wife that if there were ever a fire in the home, she should first remove the children and then, if there were time, save my scriptures and not worry about anything else.

The president and I had much to discuss as we were to be together only that evening. However, I felt a strong impression that we must do all in our power to recover the scriptures. After supper, all present knelt in prayer once again. We determined to search the immediate area near the mission office and a nearby field, hoping that the thief or thieves might have kept only the salable items and discarded the books because they were in English.

In the prayer we pleaded that the scriptures would be returned, that the persons who had taken them would be led to know of their unrighteous act and repent, and that the return of the books would be the means of bringing someone into the true church.

Eight to ten of us then loaded into the van with flashlights and warm clothing and drove to the mission office in the central city. We scoured vacant lots across the street, and adjacent streets and alleys; we talked with guards and anyone else we could find and exhausted all possibilities. No one had seen or heard anything. Finally we returned home, dejected, able only to pray individually and wait. President Allred and I worked late into the night to finish our business, and the next day Sister Cook and I flew back to Quito, Ecuador, where we lived.

During the next few weeks, the missionaries searched the lots again. They looked in hedges and garbage cans, searched a nearby park, placed a sign on a wall near where the books were stolen, requesting their return, and kept a watchful eye to see if the books might show up in some unexpected place nearby. In sheer desperation, trying to do all in their power, the missionaries decided to place an ad in two daily newspapers, offering a reward and giving explicit information concerning the books.

In Quito, Ecuador, I went through a spiritual struggle that was a very difficult one for me. For nearly three weeks, I had not studied the scriptures at all. I had tried on numerous occasions, but every time I read a verse I recalled only a few of the many cross-references I had made over the past twenty years. I was disheartened, depressed, and had no desire whatsoever to read. I prayed many times, expressing to the Father that I had never tried to use my scriptures for any purpose other than glorifying his name and trying to teach others the truths that he had taught me. I pleaded with him to do whatever had to be done in order to have them returned. My wife and little children prayed incessantly for the same blessing. Even after two or three weeks they continued praying every day, "Heavenly Father, please bring back Daddy's scriptures."

After about three weeks, I felt a strong spiritual impression: "Elder Cook, how long will you go on without reading and studying?" It seemed to me to be a test or a trial and to have something to do with the "cost" of the blessing I desired. The words burned, and I determined that I must be humble and submissive enough to start all over again. With my wife's permission to use her scriptures, I began reading in Genesis in the Old Testament, marking and cross-referencing once again.

On August 18, a friend, Brother Ebbie Davis, arrived in Ecuador from Bolivia and laid my scriptures on my desk along with a manila folder that contained the papers that I had written in Cochabamba and some recently prepared mission budgets that were also stolen. He indicated that they were the only things recovered, that he had been given those items by the mission president in La Paz as he boarded the plane, and that he did not know how the books were found, but that I would be told when I arrived there in the next few days to tour the mission.

The joy I experienced that day is indescribable! To realize that my Heavenly Father could, in some miraculous way, lift those books out of the hands of thieves in a city like La Paz and return them intact, with not one page removed, torn, or soiled, is still a miracle to me. How the faith of our family and many Bolivian missionaries was rewarded! That day I promised my Father that I would make better use of my scriptures and my time as instruments in his hands for teaching the gospel.

On Sunday, August 21, I flew to Guayaquil, Ecuador, and on to La Paz, Bolivia, arriving on August 22. Upon arrival I was given the following account:

A woman had been in one of La Paz's hundreds of marketplaces. She saw a drunk man waving a black book around. She had a strong spiritual impression that something holy was being desecrated. She approached the man and asked him what the book was. He did not know but showed it to her. She asked if he had anything else. He pulled out another black book. She asked if there were more. He removed a folder full of papers that he said he was going to burn. She offered to purchase those things from him, to which he agreed, for the price of 50 pesos, or about $2.50 in U.S. currency.

After the purchase had been made, she felt totally taken aback by what she had done. She realized the books and papers were in English—she didn't speak, read, or understand English—

and she had no desire to have any English books. She had paid nearly 10 percent of her monthly income to buy some books in a language she could not read. She immediately began to search for the church that was named in the front of the books. After approaching a number of other churches, she finally arrived at the mission office in La Paz, directed by the hand of the Lord. She had not heard of the reward nor of the ad in the newspaper, which was to appear that very day. She did not ask for any money, not even to reclaim the 50 pesos that she had paid for the books and papers. The elders received the books and folder with rejoicing and paid her the reward anyway.

She told the missionaries that she was associated with a Pentecostal sect, but she listened very intently as they unfolded the gospel to her. She recalled reading something about Joseph Smith from a pamphlet she had picked up in the street two or three years earlier. After their first discussion with her, they reported, "She is a golden contact." After the second discussion, she committed to baptism. Two weeks later, September 11, 1977, on a Sunday afternoon in La Paz, Bolivia, Sister Maria Cloefe Cardenas Terrazas and her son, Marco Fernando Miranda Cardenas, age twelve, were baptized into the true church of Jesus Christ by Elder Douglas Reeder.

Who could describe our deep, discouraging, depressing, disheartening, overpowering feelings of helplessness when the scriptures were lost? Who could describe our great feeling of joy and rejoicing when we saw the power of heaven revealed in this miraculous way? Our Heavenly Father does hear and answer the prayers of his sons and daughters if they exercise faith in the Lord Jesus Christ. The Lord said: "For verily I say unto you, That whosoever shall say unto this mountain, Be thou removed, and be thou cast into the sea; and shall not doubt in his heart, but shall believe that those things which he saith shall come to pass; he shall have whatsoever he saith.

"Therefore I say unto you, What things soever ye desire, when ye pray, believe that ye receive them, and ye shall have them." (Mark 11:23-24.)

The Purpose of This Book

The purpose of this book is to help you learn what faith is, how to obtain it, and how to exercise it to cause great things to occur in your life and in the lives of others. Will the Lord mark the way in your schooling, in your employment, in your marriage, in your family? He will. The Lord is full of mercy, forgiveness, patience, and long-suffering and is desirous of unlocking his treasure house of blessings to you if you are full of faith in the Lord Jesus Christ, for it is upon him that our faith must rest.

The Contents of This Book

This book is not intended to be just another reading experience. It discusses:
1. What faith is.
2. The characteristics of faith.
3. The foundations of faith.
4. How to obtain faith.
5. How to increase faith.
6. How to exercise faith.

At the end of each chapter you will find questions to ponder. I hope that you will use these questions and this book to actually increase your faith and to help you improve your life and solve your problems.

How to Read This Book

As you read, take time to ponder the questions at the ends of the chapters, perhaps referring to the scriptures to give you additional insights into answers to the study questions. You might discuss the questions and the things you are learning with your spouse, your companion, or a friend. You might teach the principles discussed in the book to someone else, such as your family, so that they might benefit from your discussions and so that you will better understand and internalize the principles of faith. Finally, before you begin this book, you might think of a specific problem you would like to solve or a goal you would like to reach. Then, as you read, look for ideas that might help you with your problem or goal, and listen for the promptings of the Spirit of the Lord. Follow those promptings, and the Lord will give you further light and knowledge, and you will learn what it means to exercise faith in the Lord Jesus Christ.

Learning to exercise faith is a spiritual, not a natural, process. King Benjamin said, "The natural man is an enemy to God, and has been from the fall of Adam, and will be, forever and ever, unless he yields to the enticings of the Holy Spirit, and putteth off the natural man and becometh a saint through the atonement of Christ the Lord." (Mosiah 3:19.)

We hear much about what the world teaches about positive attitude, but faith is much more than that. We are talking about becoming a true Latter-day Saint, full of faith in the Lord Jesus Christ.

For that reason, I would like to make one more suggestion about how to read this book. I believe with all my heart that the Lord is our true trainer and teacher. As you read and ponder the principles discussed in this book, please pray many times in your heart, "Heavenly Father, please bless me that I may understand the principle of faith. Thou knowest me. Thou knowest my needs right now. Please help me understand these principles and how I may apply them in my life."

I bear humble witness to you in the name of Jesus Christ, that if you will do that, if you will pray intently a number of times as you read, the Lord will speak to you in your heart, for he, not this book, is our true teacher. As you continue to pray, he will permanently change some things inside of you. And he will open your mind as to what you ought to do with a wayward child, a troubled friend, or an investigator with whom you are working. He will help you solve your problems at home, at church, at work, or at school. He will help you learn to live by the power of faith.

Questions to Ponder

1. What was the first step taken to find the missing scriptures? Have you taken this step in obtaining your righteous desires?

_____

_____

_____

2. What other steps were taken to find the scriptures? What other steps can you take?

_____

_____

_____

3. What was the "cost" the Lord required in returning the missing scriptures? Do you feel in your heart that there is a "cost" for the blessings you desire that you have not yet paid? What do you need to do to pay it?

_____

_____

_____

4. What spiritual and temporal blessings arose from the experience of the missing scriptures? What blessings do you see as a result of the things you are doing to exercise your faith?

_____

_____

_____

5. What does the Lord say we must do to obtain our righteous desires?

_____

_____

_____

6. What suggestions are given in the introduction about how to get the most from this book? Which of these suggestions do you feel would be of most help to you?

_____

_____

_____

7. List one challenge on which you might concentrate your faith while reading, pondering, and practicing the principles of faith about which you will now read.

_____

_____

_____

Chapter Two

What Faith Is

When I was president of the Uruguay/Paraguay Mission, I met a great missionary, a young man full of faith. He was an Uruguayan. He had served about three or four months in the mission when I arrived as the mission president. Wherever he and his senior companion went, they baptized. In the beginning I thought this was due to the senior companion—I thought that this particular elder was too inexperienced for such success. That was a mistake.

Eventually he was called to be a senior companion and district leader and was sent into a city that had gained a reputation of being a tough, tough place. The missionaries had not baptized anyone there for about nine months or a year—not one person! Only ten or twelve members were attending the branch when we sent this elder there with two other elders and his companion. I didn't tell him anything—I just sent him the notice of change of assignment. After only three weeks he began baptizing—he baptized four or five during those three weeks. After he had been there about ten weeks, all the missionaries started baptizing.

Finally he was called to be a zone leader because he had such an ability to teach others, and we sent him in to a large, extended zone. That zone involved the whole upper area of the country, and there were some difficult cities up there. We thought that it

11

would be a challenge for him because now he would have to teach all the missionaries to do what he was doing, and he would have to do it through district leaders, which would be a new challenge for him. We left him there two or three months, and they baptized multitudes. He and his companion, and the Spirit, of course, changed that whole zone—all the member leaders and everyone else—into "a new people."

Then in November I began struggling—the Lord wanted to tell me something. I began to get a restless feeling about this elder, and the feeling was, "Send him to Paraguay." The elders were having little success in Paraguay—hardly baptizing anyone. They were averaging only twenty or twenty-five baptisms a month in the whole country. The feeling came to transfer this elder to Paraguay, and I wrestled with that and thought, "He has really proved himself here, but to put him in Paraguay might just drag him down. He may have a hard time holding on there." I had to struggle with my faith to convince myself that he really ought to go. But when those feelings come you have to listen. We sent him a telegram telling him that he was transferred to Asuncion, Paraguay, as the zone leader, and that he was leaving the next day.

On December 1 he came in and then left the mission home without my seeing him, but he left a letter, which said, "Dear President Cook, I received a telegram today telling me to go to Paraguay, and I thought you ought to know a few things: (1) You can't baptize in Paraguay. I have had at least ten or fifteen elders tell me their experiences there. (2) The members are not helping at all. (3) There are great chastity problems. . . ." He named ten or twelve of the most negative things I had ever heard, and I thought, "Oh no, negative people have got to him!" But as he finished the list he said, "I just wanted you to know, President, that I don't believe one of those things." Talk about faith! And then he said, "I want you to know that on Christmas Day we are going to baptize twenty-five people." Christmas was only twenty-five days away, and when I read that I thought, "The Lord bless you. You have a tremendous amount of faith if you can do that. You don't know the country—you haven't even been there. You don't know where you are going to live. You don't know your companion, the leaders, or the members. You don't know anything, and yet you are telling me that you are going to baptize twenty-five people in twenty-five days."

Well this young man really was full of faith and was a fine example of a great Latin leader. On December 25 he baptized eighteen people. They hadn't reached twenty-five—they had baptized eighteen, which was about all that the whole country usually baptized in a month. It was a great privilege two weeks later, when I was in Paraguay, to participate in a baptismal service where he and his companion baptized eleven more people. His district, where he had taught the elders what to do, baptized thirty that same day.

How did this elder achieve such marvelous results? Through a charismatic personality? Through worldly techniques of persuasion? Through only a positive attitude? No, he did it through his faith in Jesus Christ.

The Savior said, "If ye have faith in me ye shall have power to do whatsoever thing is expedient in me." (Moroni 7:33.)

Using the scriptures, let's attempt to define what faith is, because that will give us a basis for understanding and developing the kind of faith this elder had.

Faith Is the Substance of Things Hoped For

Hebrews 11:1 says this:

> Now faith is the substance . . .

Joseph Smith translated the word *substance* in the inspired version to mean assurance.

> Now faith is the *assurance* of things hoped for, the evidence of things not seen. For by it the elders obtained a good report. Through faith we understand that the worlds were framed by the word of God . . . By faith Abel offered unto God a more excellent

13

sacrifice than Cain, . . . By faith Enoch was translated that he should not see death; . . . But without faith it is impossible to please him. (Heb. 11:1-6.)

This chapter gives us many great examples of faith and some great miracles that came about as a direct result of men's faith. You should carefully read and meditate upon this chapter, as it would be very beneficial for anyone who is studying the principle of faith.

Let's look at Abraham and his faith as represented in the fourth chapter of Romans. Notice carefully the process that Abraham went through:

Therefore [the promise of eternal life] is of faith, that it might be by grace; to the end the promise might be sure to all the seed; . . .

In other words, the promise of eternal life comes by faith.

. . . not to that only which is of the law, but to that also which is of the faith of Abraham; who is the father of us all, (As it is written, I have made thee a father of many nations,) . . .

Abraham had received a promise that he was going to be the father of many nations. But he got older and older, and apparently he and his wife had passed the time when it was possible for them to bear children. Did Abraham begin to waver in his faith? No, he continued to believe in the promise that was given to him that he would be the father of nations, without any evidence whatsoever that his wife was going to have a child.

. . . before him whom he believed, even God, who quickeneth the dead, and calleth those things which be not as though they were. (Verses 16-17.)

This is an interesting way of talking about the natural man. Those things that appear not to be, are. And those things that appear to be, are not. It depends on whether you look at it with your spiritual or natural eyes.

14

> Who against hope believed in hope, that he might become the father of many nations; according to that which was spoken, So shall thy seed be.
>
> And being not weak in faith, he considered not his own body now dead, when he was about an hundred years old, . . .

It might be easy to read that and go on, but I imagine that if you were a hundred years old, it would take a bit of faith to believe that after all that time you were still going to have a son. But he believed.

> \. . . neither yet the deadness of Sara's womb: . . .

To compound the problem, Sara was ninety years old. The promise might have been easier to believe if Sara had been in her thirties, but she wasn't. That would have looked like an impossible situation to the natural man.

> He staggered not at the promise of God through unbelief; . . .

This man was a great example. He believed, in spite of all the odds against him, in the promises of God.

> . . . but was strong in faith, giving glory to God; . . .

We must always be sure not to take any glory unto ourselves.

> . . . And being fully persuaded that, what he had promised, he was able also to perform. (Verses 18-21.)

In other words, Abraham believed that the Lord could deliver and would. We also must believe this. If we go forth in faith, doing our part, the Lord will provide.

> And therefore it was imputed to him for righteousness. (Verse 22.)

Of course, the son was born, but another challenge came to Abraham even after that. When it came time to sacrifice his son, Abraham still believed—right to the very moment when he was going to snuff out the life of his boy. Abraham had an unshakable inner assurance of the promise of endless posterity that he hoped for.

Faith Is the Principle of Action in All Intelligent Beings

The definition of faith as given in the *Lectures on Faith* seems to center around two basic descriptions of faith that are really one. First of all, it is centered around the fact that faith is the moving cause of all action in all intelligent beings. The exact words are: "As faith is the moving cause of all action in temporal concerns, so it is in spiritual." (*Lectures on Faith* 1:12.) The lectures also say that all intelligent beings function that way.

> Faith is the assurance which men have of the existence of things which they have not seen, and the principle of action in all intelligent beings. If men were duly to consider themselves, and turn their thoughts and reflections to the operations of their own minds, they would readily discover that it is faith, and faith only, which is the moving cause of all action in them; that without it both mind and body would be in a state of inactivity, and all their exertions would cease, both physical and mental. (*Lectures on Faith*, 1:9-10.)

Let me give you an example or two of how literal this is and how inclusive it is of every act performed here on earth—by good men, by bad men, by women and children, and even by every intelligent being. Do you think I would have written this book if I had thought no one would ever read it? Never. Do you think that if a pedestrian were quite certain that he could not make it across the street that he would ever attempt to cross? No, he would not. Think about every single thing that you do, and you will come to the conclusion that there is no action among men that is not born of faith. That action will result in the fruit that is desired—for good or for evil. If a person desires something evil and believes that he can get it, (and we are not talking about faith in the Lord now, but only about faith in a general sense) he can obtain it by his faith or belief that he can. There are many who have.

So remember first of all that faith truly is the moving cause of all action in intelligent beings. I am going to quote just one more short paragraph from the *Lectures on Faith:*

> Would you have ever sown, if you had not believed that you would reap? Would you have ever planted, if you had not believed that you would gather? Would you have ever asked, unless you had believed that you would receive? Would you have ever sought, unless you had believed that you would have found? Or, would you have ever knocked, unless you had believed that it would have been opened unto you? In a word, is there anything that you would have done, either physical or mental, if you had not previously believed? Are not all your exertions of every kind, dependent on your faith? Or, may we not ask, what have you, or what do you possess, which you have not obtained by reason of your faith? (*Lectures on Faith* 1:11.)

The lectures say later on that our food, raiment, lodging, and all we have come as a result of that kind of faith. As I understand it, that applies to all people, good or evil, who have faith that if they do "these" things, "this" will happen. There are many who have become very rich, even millionaires, because they have learned some of the things that relate distantly to faith. They have used some of those principles, which they have found to be true, and made them work for them, and they have been temporally successful.

I remember hearing from different missionaries that faith is having a positive attitude. That is both true and false. It is true in the sense that a man full of faith will have a positive attitude, but it doesn't mean that he who has a positive attitude is necessarily full of faith (of the kind that we are talking about, which is faith in the Lord). They can be totally unrelated. Nevertheless, faith in one form or another is the principle of action in all intelligent beings. A question you might ask yourself is, "Are my everyday actions based on faith in the Lord or in something else?"

Faith Is Power

Faith in the Lord is different from any other kind of faith. Faith is power. In the *Lectures on Faith* we find this:

> As faith is the moving cause of all action in temporal concerns, so it is in spiritual; for the Saviour has said, and that truly, that "He

17

that *believeth* and is baptized, shall be saved." (Mark 16:16; italics added.)

As we receive by faith all temporal blessings that we do receive, so we in like manner receive by faith all spiritual blessings that we do receive. But faith is not only the principle of action, but of power also, in all intelligent beings, whether in heaven or on earth. Thus says the author of the epistle to the Hebrews, [11:3].

"Through faith we understand that the worlds were framed by the word of God; so that things which are seen were not made of things which do appear." (*Lectures on Faith* 1:12-14.)

When we talk about faith, sometimes we think only of belief, or of straining our mind to believe in something. But the *Lectures on Faith* talk about faith as being a literal power. In this definition of faith we find these words:

Faith, then, is the first great governing principle which has power, dominion, and authority over all things; by it they exist, by it they are upheld, by it they are changed, or by it they remain, agreeable to the will of God. Without it there is no power, and without power there could be no creation nor existence. (*Lectures on Faith* 1:24.)

The *Lectures* also note:

Had it not been for the principle of faith the worlds would never have been framed, neither would man have been formed of the dust. It is the principle by which Jehovah works, and through which he exercises power over all temporal as well as eternal things. Take this principle or attribute—for it is an attribute— from the Deity, and he would cease to exist. (*Lectures on Faith* 1:16.)

Now, you think about faith in that overall sense, that it is literally the power by which God himself operates. It makes you realize that when someone says, "I have got to study other things now, because I have already studied the first principles of the gospel," he is a long way from even beginning to understand a small part of the first principle of the gospel—faith in the Lord Jesus Christ.

Faith is much more than just a positive attitude or any of the many techniques that man has learned to use to achieve his desires. True faith is in the Lord Jesus Christ unto life and salvation. There are many in the world who have their faith in worldly things, their positive attitude, but it will never take them anywhere. They have never come to understand that faith does have power, dominion, and authority over all things. It is the very power by which God himself operates.

Questions to Ponder

1. How was the young elder able to baptize so many people?

_____

_____

_____

2. How did the elder react to the negative things he had heard about Paraguay? What can you do to eliminate negative thoughts about your goals?

_____

_____

_____

3. What did the elder actually do in his mind to be able to exercise faith? What can you do to do the same thing?

_____

_____

_____

4. What are the three definitions of faith given in this chapter?

_____

_____

_____

5. How was Abraham able to believe the promise of the Lord in spite of such apparently great odds that the promise was impossible?

_____

_____

_____

6. What seemingly insurmountable obstacles face you? What can you do to go forward in spite of these obstacles?

_____

_____

_____

7. If by faith God organizes and sustains his creations, how can you do the same in your sphere?

_____

_____

_____

8. In what things can you as a parent, spouse, employee, teacher, leader, or missionary begin to exercise your faith?

_____

_____

_____

9. How can knowing what faith is help you to live by faith?

_____

_____

_____

Chapter Three

Characteristics of Faith

One morning our family was talking at the breakfast table. We had finished our scripture reading, and I was trying to teach the children something. I had set things up so that they would ask me a question and then say, "Oh Dad, tell us about it." And that's just what happened. So I said, "Well, I am glad that you asked!" Then I asked them, "Do you believe what I am going to teach you now?" And then one of the older boys, who was nine at the time, just as quickly as he could get it out, said, "Dad, we believe all of the words that you tell us." I don't know anything greater that a man could hear from his son.

The Lord told Alma, "Blessed art thou, Alma, . . because of thy exceeding faith in the words alone of my servant Abinadi." (Mosiah 26:14-15.) Had an angel appeared to Alma about that time? No. He *just believed* on Abinadi's words.

Faith Is Related to Belief

A simple, childlike belief is an important characteristic of faith in the Lord. In Matthew 21:22 the Lord says, "All things, whatsoever ye shall ask in prayer, *believing*, ye shall receive.

From the words of Alma, one might better understand the power of belief:

God is merciful unto all who believe on his name; therefore he desireth, in the first place, *that ye should believe*, yea, even on his word. But behold, if ye will awake and arouse your faculties, even to an experiment upon my words, and exercise a particle of faith, yea, *even if ye can no more than desire to believe*, let this desire work in you, *even until ye believe* in a manner that ye can give place for a portion of my words. (Alma 32:22,27; italics added.)

From the words "even if ye can no more than desire to believe," it would appear that belief is the beginning of the process of acquiring faith.

The Master taught us the great power of belief in the example of the man from whose son he cast out a foul spirit.

One of the multitude . . . said, Master, I have brought unto thee my son, which hath a dumb spirit; and wheresoever he taketh him, he teareth him: and he foameth, and gnasheth with his teeth, and pineth away: and I spake to thy disciples that they should cast him out; and they could not.

He answereth him, and saith, "O faithless generation, how long shall I be with you? . . . bring him unto me.

And they brought him unto him: and when he saw him, straightway the spirit tare him; and he fell on the ground, and wallowed foaming.

And he asked his father, How long is it ago since this came unto him? And he said, Of a child. And ofttimes it hath cast him into the fire, and into the waters, to destroy him; but if thou canst do any thing, have compassion on us, and help us.

Jesus said unto him, *If thou canst believe, all things are possible to him that believeth.* And straightway the father of the child cried out, and said with tears, Lord, *I believe; help thou mine unbelief.*

When Jesus saw that the people came running together he rebuked the foul spirit, saying unto him, Thou dumb and deaf spirit, I charge thee, come out of him, and enter no more into him.

And the spirit cried, and rent him sore, and came out of him: and he was as one dead; insomuch that many said, He is dead. But Jesus took him by the hand, and lifted him up and he arose. (Mark 9:17-27; italics added.)

We see from this story that simple belief is an integral part of having faith.

Faith Is Related to Hope

Moroni gave a good explanation of the relationship between faith and hope:

> I would speak unto you concerning hope. How is it that ye can attain unto faith, save ye shall have hope? (Moroni 7:40.)

This teaches us that we must first have hope and then comes faith. If you were to read further, in verse 42 you would see that the Lord reverses that and says we must first have faith or we cannot even have any hope. This helps us understand that faith and hope are closely interrelated. In verse 41 we are told what to hope for, and it is once again very interesting as it all relates to the Lord:

> And what is it that ye shall hope for?

That is a good question. What is it we should have faith in? What is it that we should hope for?

> Behold I say unto you that ye shall have hope through the atonement of Christ and the power of his resurrection, to be raised unto life eternal, and this because of your faith in him according to the promise. Wherefore, if a man have faith he must needs have hope; for without faith there cannot be any hope. (Moroni 7:41-42.)

Faith and hope truly are interrelated, as is suggested in the wellknown sentence in Hebrews 11:1.

> Faith is the substance of things *hoped for*, the evidence of things *not seen*. (Italics added.)

This is also mentioned in Ether 12:4.

> Whoso believeth in God might *with surety hope* for a better world, yea, even a place at the right hand of God, *which hope cometh of faith*, maketh an anchor to the souls of men, which would make them sure and steadfast, always abounding in good works, being led to glorify God. (Italics added.)

Faith Is Not Associated with Doubt and Fear

Faith in the Lord is not associated with doubt and fear. The *Lectures on Faith* state:

> Such is the weakness of man, and such his frailties, that he is liable to sin continually, and if God were not long-suffering, and full of compassion, gracious and merciful, and of a forgiving disposition, man would be cut off from before him, in consequence of which he would *be in continual doubt and could not exercise faith; for where doubt is, there faith has no power;* but by man's believing that God is full of compassion and forgiveness, long-suffering and slow to anger, *he can exercise faith in him and overcome doubt,* so as to be exceedingly strong. (Questions and answers on Lecture 3.)

It is evident that a man who has continual doubt cannot exercise faith, for where doubt is, there faith has no power. The Lord indicated in the Doctrine and Covenants 6:34, 36 the following:

> Therefore, fear not, little flock; do good; let earth and hell combine against you, for if ye are built upon my rock, they cannot prevail. . . . Look unto me in *every thought; doubt not, fear not.* (Italics added.)

We can see that in order to not fear, we must look unto the Lord in every thought. The Lord will uphold and sustain us in the things we are righteously striving to accomplish.

We can see this principle at work in the account of Christ walking on the sea and the Apostle Peter attempting to do the same. The scriptures record:

> In the fourth watch of the night Jesus went unto them, walking on the sea. And when the disciples saw him walking on the sea, they were troubled, saying, It is a spirit; and *they cried out for fear.* But straightway Jesus spake unto them, saying, Be of good cheer; it is I; *be not afraid.*
>
> And Peter answered him and said, Lord, if it be thou, bid me come unto thee on the water. And he said, Come. And when Peter was come down out of the ship, he walked on the water, to go to Jesus. But when he saw the wind boisterous, *he was afraid;* and beginning to sink, he cried, saying, Lord, save me. And immediately Jesus stretched forth his hand, and caught him, and said unto him,

O thou of little faith, wherefore didst thou doubt? (Matthew 14: 25-31; italics added.)

Note that Peter, in the moment that he realized that he was actually walking on the water, was afraid. And once the fear came, he began to sink, and he lost the power that he was exercising temporarily.

Doubt and faith cannot exist within a person at the same time. James also teaches us this great lesson:

If any of you lack wisdom, let him ask of God, that giveth to all men liberally, and upbraideth not; and it shall be given to him. *But let him ask in faith, nothing wavering.* For he that wavereth is like a wave of the sea driven with the wind and tossed. *For let not that man think that he shall receive anything of the Lord.* (James 1:5-7; italics added.)

In Mark 11:23-24 we read:

Verily I say unto you, That whosoever shall say unto this mountain, Be thou removed, and be thou cast into the sea; *and shall not doubt in his heart, but shall believe that those things which he saith shall come to pass;* he shall have whatsoever he saith.

Therefore I say unto you, What things soever ye desire, when ye pray, *believe that ye receive them,* and ye shall have them. (Italics added.)

If a person will not doubt in his heart, but believe that those things that he says shall come to pass, they truly will come to pass. If you believe, you will receive. Are you striving to believe in God and to cast out your doubts, fears, and negative thoughts?

Faith Makes People Sure and Steadfast

Moroni wrote,

Whoso believeth in God might with surety hope for a better world, yea, even a place at the right hand of God, which hope cometh of faith, maketh an anchor to the souls of men, which would make them sure and steadfast.

Moroni is attempting to describe what faith will do—it will

make you sure and steadfast. He is not talking about the way of the world in being sure, but being *spiritually* sure.

Faith Does Not Come by Signs

There is another characteristic of faith that we need to understand before we try to apply it. Faith is not based on signs. The Lord has said:

> The gospel must be preached unto every creature, *with signs following them that believe.* (D&C 58:64; italics added.)
> And he that *believeth* and is baptized shall be saved, and he that believeth not shall be damned.
> And he *that believeth* shall be blest with signs following, even as it is written. (D&C 68:9-10; italics added.)

Signs come by faith, but signs must come in the Lord's way. The Lord told Joseph Smith:

> He that seeketh signs shall see signs, but not unto salvation.
> Verily, I say unto you, there are those among you who seek signs, and there have been such even from the beginning.

I would suggest that each of us is guilty of this to a degree. We might even be seeking for a sign and not be aware of it. It is a refinement of the Spirit to know the difference. The Lord continued:

> But, behold, faith cometh not by signs, but signs follow those that believe.
> Yea, signs come by faith, not by the will of men, nor as they please, but by the will of God. (D&C 63:7-10.)

Remember well that signs do not produce faith. Some people think that if an angel appeared unto them, they would believe and have faith, and that after he left they would keep all of the commandments. Those are the teachings of the natural man, and they are not true. Faith is born inside. Faith comes by the Spirit of God, not by signs.

Remember not to confuse gifts of the Spirit with signs. We are counseled by the Lord, "Seek earnestly the best gifts." (D&C 46:8.) Many of these gifts are listed in the Doctrine and Covenants. (See D&C 46:9-33.) Spiritual gifts can come by the will of man through faith. Signs come by the will of God and follow faith.

Faith Is Not a Perfect Knowledge

When Joseph Smith left the grove, was his faith that God existed weak? That is ridiculous, isn't it? He left with a sure knowledge that the Father and the Son lived. If he *knew* that, he no longer had faith in it. He had faith in many other things, but he had a sure knowledge that God lived. Alma explained this principle in this way:

> Faith is not to have a perfect knowledge of things; therefore if ye have faith ye hope for things which are not seen, which are true. (Alma 32:21.)

Then he goes on to say:

> Now, as I said concerning faith—that it was not a perfect knowledge—even so it is with my words. Ye cannot know of their surety at first, unto perfection, any more than faith is a perfect knowledge.
>
> Now, we will compare the word unto a seed. Now, if ye give place, that a seed may be planted in your heart, behold, if it be a true seed, or a good seed, *if ye do not cast it out by your unbelief*, that ye will resist the Spirit of the Lord, behold, it will begin to swell within your breasts; and when you feel these swelling motions, ye will begin to say within yourselves—It must needs be that this is a good seed, or that the word is good, for [1] it beginneth to enlarge my soul; [2] yea, it beginneth to enlighten my understanding, [3] yea, it beginneth to be delicious to me.
>
> Now behold, would not this increase your faith? I say unto you, Yea; nevertheless it hath not grown up to a perfect knowledge. (Alma 32:26-29; italics added.)

This chapter continues to talk about the seed and its growth. In verse 34 we read:

> And now, behold, is your knowledge perfect? Yea, your knowledge is perfect in that thing, and your faith is dormant; and this because ye know, for ye know that the word hath swelled your

souls, and ye also know that it hath sprouted up, that your understanding doth begin to be enlightened, and your mind doth begin to expand.

Alma explains beautifully some of the characteristics of faith. As we study these characteristics, we need to remember that faith is something we know very little about. The Lord says that if we have the faith of a mustard seed, we can say to a mountain, "Remove hence to yonder place," and it would remove. (Matthew 17:20.) This teaches me that I must have something less than that, perhaps, and that I know very little about it. Thus, I continue the search to understand what it means to have faith in the Lord Jesus Christ. I hope that you, too, will take this as a beginning point to greater study, meditation, and prayer to understand faith in the Lord Jesus Christ. As you do so, the Lord will reveal to you further knowledge about these important principles, for he has promised, "If thou shalt ask, thou shalt receive revelation upon revelation, knowledge upon knowledge, that thou mayest know the mysteries and peaceable things—that which bringeth joy, that which bringeth life eternal." (D&C 42:61.)

Questions to Ponder

1. How is faith related to belief?

_____

_____

_____

2. How is faith related to hope?

_____

_____

_____

3. How is faith related to signs?

_____

_____

_____

4. How is faith related to spiritual gifts?

_____

_____

_____

5. How is faith related to knowledge?

_____

_____

_____

6. How do doubt and fear affect faith?

_____

_____

_____

7. What can you do to increase your belief and your hope that your righteous desires will come to pass?

_____

_____

_____

8. What can you do to increase your faith by increasing your knowledge?

_____

_____

_____

9. What can you do to cast out your doubts and fears?

_____

_____

_____

Chapter Four

Foundations of Faith

When I was in Venezuela a few years ago, a number of the Latter-day Saints and many non-Mormons were talking about a prophecy made by a woman in Europe. She had prophesied that Caracas, which at that time was a city of over three million people, would be destroyed the following day. Many people believed, and thousands of them left Caracas the day I arrived. The following day there was no destruction, and I heard some talk among the Church members that went something like this: "I knew it wasn't going to happen—we didn't leave the city." They had exercised their faith that this woman was wrong by *staying* in Caracas. What worried me was their reasoning. They said, "We know the Lord wouldn't do anything like that to Caracas because we have a stake here now." One person said, "I know that if the city really was going to be destroyed, the Lord would have revealed it to Elder Cook or to the mission or stake presidents so that the Saints could have been evacuated out of the city." Another one said, "If the Lord didn't reveal it to one of the local leaders he would have revealed it to President Kimball." Now that is pretty shaky reasoning; anyone who has read the scriptures knows that the Lord allows evil to come upon the good as well as the wicked. We must be careful not to second-guess the Lord.

Once in Colombia we were having a tremendous problem

31

getting visas so that missionaries could come into the country. One woman said, "I know this is not the will of the Lord—he wants missionary work to go forward, and if we had enough faith, he would not allow the government to withhold the visas. If we had enough faith, we could solve this problem." Now that sounds reasonable, doesn't it? But it may or may not have been true. I think one of the greatest blessings Mexico had was when their government would not allow North American missionaries to enter Mexico for a time. Young Mexicans then began to serve missions in their own country, because there was no other alternative. Then, while all the North American missionaries called to Mexico waited but could not enter, language training began. *Then* was born the idea of a language training center, which shortly came into being. It was later called the Missionary Training Center. The Lord has his own purposes. He will do things in his own way. He can bring miraculous things from one seemingly small incident or even from adversity.

The *Lectures on Faith* note that there are three elements upon which true faith in the Lord is based:

> Three things are necessary in order that any rational and intelligent being may exercise faith in God unto life and salvation.
> First, the idea that he actually exists.
> Secondly, a *correct* idea of his character, perfections, and attributes.
> Thirdly, an actual knowledge that the course of life which he is pursuing is according to his will. (*Lectures on Faith* 3:2-5.)

If your faith is based in these elements, then you will have sufficient faith to be able to exercise true faith in the Lord unto life and salvation.

1. The Idea That God Actually Exists

The natural man, looking at the first element of faith might quickly say, "Let's go on to the next principle, because I already know that God exists." But the spiritually attuned person understands how very little he knows about something even this basic. We know in different ways and in varying degrees that God exists, and here we are taught something beyond what we usually think about.

God's Creations Testify of Him

Coming to know that God exists centers in perhaps two main principles or ideas, the first being that God's creations themselves testify that he exists. The Lord has said:

> The earth rolls upon her wings, and the sun giveth his light by day, and the moon giveth her light by night, and the stars also give their light, as they roll upon their wings in their glory, in the midst of the power of God.
>
> Unto what shall I liken these kingdoms, that ye may understand?
>
> Behold, all these are kingdoms, and *any man who hath seen any or the least of these hath seen God* moving in his majesty and power. (D&C 88:45-47; italics added.)

The Lord has blessed us with sufficient perception to recognize in the creations a witness that he lives, so that anyone could have faith and believe on his name. All over the world men and women believe in some kind of superior being who created the heavens and the earth. They do not know what he is or who he is, but they at least believe in him. That is a great witness to me that the Lord set things up so that with nothing but his creations, we could have faith that he exists.

The Lord told Adam:

> All things are created and made to bear record of me, both things which are temporal, and things which are spiritual; things which are in the heavens above, and things which are on the earth, and things which are in the earth, and things which are under the earth, both above and beneath: all things *bear record of me.* (Moses 6:63; italics added.)

And Alma told Korihor:

> *All things denote there is a God;* yea, even the earth, and all things that are upon the face of it, yea, and its motion, yea, and also all the planets which move in their regular form do witness that there is a Supreme Creator. (Alma 30:44; italics added.)

Alma testified that the Lord organized the elements in such a way that all things testify of God to his children.

Others Testify of God

Secondly, the Lord uses the testimony of others in order that mankind might believe in him. The day that Joseph Smith walked out of the Sacred Grove, there was a man on earth who had seen for himself that God truly lives. He had been motivated by faith to go to the grove to pray, but when he walked out of the grove, he had a perfect knowledge that God lives. That experience gave him power to say this:

> I had actually seen a light, and in the midst of that light I saw two Personages, and they did in reality speak to me; and though I was hated and persecuted for saying that I had seen a vision, yet it was true; and while they were persecuting me, reviling me, and speaking all manner of evil against me falsely for so saying, I was led to say in my heart: Why persecute me for telling the truth? I have actually seen a vision; and who am I that I can withstand God, or why does the world think to make me deny what I have actually seen? For *I had seen a vision; I knew it, and I knew that God knew it,* and I could not deny it, neither dared I do it; at least I knew that by so doing I would offend God, and come under condemnation." (Joseph Smith—History 1:25; italics added.)

Joseph Smith's testimony has become a basis of faith for millions of people throughout the world. The *Lectures on Faith* note:

> We have . . . clearly set forth how it is, and how it was, that God became an object of faith for rational beings; and also, upon what foundation the testimony was based which excited the inquiry and diligent search of the ancient saints to seek after and obtain a knowledge of the glory of God; and *we have seen that it was human testimony, and human testimony only, that excited this inquiry,* in the first instance, in their minds. *It was the credence they gave to the testimony of their fathers, this testimony having aroused their minds to inquire after the knowledge of God;* the inquiry frequently terminated, indeed always terminated when rightly pursued, in the most glorious discoveries and eternal certainty. (*Lectures on Faith* 2:56; italics added.)

After that first great vision, men began to believe on the words of the Prophet Joseph Smith, and faith once again began to spread throughout the earth. The Lord began the process exactly the same way with Adam. In Moses 5:58-59 we read:

> The Gospel began to be preached, from the beginning, being declared *by holy angels* sent forth from the presence of God, and *by his own voice*, and *by the gift of the Holy Ghost.*
>
> And thus all things were confirmed unto Adam, by an holy ordinance, and the Gospel preached, and a decree sent forth, that it should be in the world, until the end thereof; and thus it was. Amen. (Moses 5:58-59; italics added.)

Adam saw God. He walked and talked with him and heard his voice. And from Adam and Eve came the testimony of God to others:

> And Adam and Eve blessed the name of God, and they *made all things known unto their sons and their daughters.* (Moses 5:12; italics added.)

Mormon said this:

> Now I come to that faith, of which I said I would speak; and I will tell you the way whereby ye may lay hold on every good thing.
>
> For behold, God knowing all things, being from everlasting to everlasting, behold, *he sent angels* to minister unto the children of men, to make manifest concerning the coming of Christ; and in Christ there should come every good thing. (Moroni 7:22; italics added.)

In other words, the Lord sent angels to testify of him so that men could behold with their eyes and be sure witnesses that God does live.

> *God also declared unto prophets*, by his own mouth, that Christ should come.
>
> And behold, there were divers ways that he did manifest things unto the children of men, which were good; and all things which are good cometh of Christ; otherwise men were fallen, and there could no good thing come unto them.

Wherefore, by the ministering of angels, and by every word which proceeded forth out of the mouth of God, men began to exercise faith in Christ; and thus by faith, they did lay hold upon every good thing; and thus it was until the coming of Christ.

And after that he came men also were saved by faith in his name; and by faith, they become the sons of God. And as sure as Christ liveth he spake these words unto our fathers, saying; Whatsoever thing ye shall ask the Father in my name, which is good, in faith believing that ye shall receive, behold, it shall be done unto you. (Moroni 7:23-26; italics added.)

Later Mormon said this:

Neither have angels ceased to minister unto the children of men.

For behold, they are subject unto him, to minister according to the word of his command, showing themselves unto them of strong faith and a firm mind in every form of godliness.

And the office of their ministry is to call men unto repentance and to fulfill and to do the work of the covenants of the Father, which he hath made unto the children of men, to prepare the way among the children of men, by *declaring the word of Christ unto the chosen vessels of the Lord, that they may bear testimony of him.*

And by so doing, the Lord God prepareth the way that *the residue of men may have faith in Christ, that the Holy Ghost may have place in their hearts, according to the power thereof;* and after this manner bringeth to pass the Father, the covenants which he hath made unto the children of men.

And Christ hath said: *If ye will have faith in me ye shall have power to do whatsoever thing is expedient in me.* (Moroni 7:29-33; italics added.)

As you hear someone's testimony, your faith has a chance to increase. Your faith in the fact that God lives begins to grow and develop. Think of the words of Paul: "Faith cometh by hearing, and hearing by the word of God." (Romans 10:17.) Some ask, "Do we really need to attend our meetings? Do we need to go where the servants of the Lord are preaching the gospel?" My answer would be, "If you want your faith to increase, you need to be there."

Take some time to try to answer the question "Who is God?" or "What is God to me?" Really take a few minutes right now and think about that before you go on reading. When we ask that question, the natural man in us would tend to name the more physical things. We might say, "God is a perfected man. He was resurrected as Jesus was. He is a glorified being. He is different from the Holy Ghost, who is just a spirit." We might begin to name those things. But they are things only *about* God. But then afterward, we might begin to think something like this: "I remember an experience when I was younger that taught me that God does love everyone and is no respecter of persons. And I know he loves me, because he has answered my prayers." As you think about those kinds of things, you will come to a better understanding of who God is and how much you may or may not know about him. It is a very different thing to say you know Jesus is the Christ and to really *know Jesus.*

2. A Correct Idea of God's Character, Perfections, and Attributes

The second element of faith is to have a correct idea concerning God's characteristics, perfections, and attributes.

At times people have come to me to confess some type of transgression and have said something like, "I know that the Lord will have a hard time forgiving me." This has helped me realize that such a person does not yet know his Father in heaven as he attempts to describe to me what the Lord is or is not going to do. I have found that I, too, know very little about my Father in heaven. As I have thought about him, I have asked myself, "How do I learn more?" I would like to give you a few suggestions.

Know God through Prayer

Prayer is one of the best ways to come to know the Lord—not just saying your prayers but really praying, conversing with the Lord. If a person will do this he can know the Lord, because the Lord will reveal knowledge of his ways to him. Jacob said this:

> Great and marvelous are the works of the Lord. How unsearchable are the depths of the mysteries of him; and it is impossible that man should find out all his ways. And no man knoweth of his ways *save it be revealed unto him;* wherefore, brethren, despise not the revelations of God. (Jacob 4:8; italics added.)

That is the only way you can get such knowledge—by revelation from him.

Know God through the Scriptures

I would suggest another way to better know the Lord: an intense, continual, and prayerful search to know him through the scriptures. The Lord has revealed in the scriptures much of what we need to know about his characteristics, perfections, and attributes.

The Lord told Martin Harris through the Prophet Joseph Smith, "Learn of me, and listen to my words; walk in the meekness of my Spirit, and you shall have peace in me." (D&C 19:23.) Samuel, the Lamanite, noted that many of the Nephites were "led to believe the holy scriptures, . . . which leadeth them to faith on the Lord." (Helaman 15:7.) Studying the scriptures is a powerful way to learn to know the Lord and develop faith in him.

Know God through Intense Observation

I would suggest that a third way to know God is to observe closely everything that goes on around you, seeking after revelation. Brigham Young once said that revelations come from many sources: the Lord, the Lord's servants, other men, the Lord's creations, and many other things. Revelations are not confined to any one person. The Lord's revelations concerning the government of his church are confined to the leaders of the Church, but other revelations are wide open for anyone to receive. Some of the greatest knowledge that the Lord has blessed me with has come by closely observing others and watching how they act and react. This teaches me sometimes what the Lord is and other times what he is not. A spark of divinity, the light of Christ, is in everyone and everything, and if you keenly observe God's creations, you will learn about him.

Characteristics of God

The *Lectures on Faith* teach us the following about God:

> We here observe that God is the only supreme governor and independent being in whom all fullness and perfection dwell; who is omnipotent, omnipresent and omniscient; without beginning of days or end of life; and that in him every good gift and every good principle dwell; and that he is the Father of lights; in him the principle of faith dwells independently, and he is the object in whom the faith of all other rational and accountable beings center for life and salvation. (*Lectures on Faith* 2:2.)

The lectures teach from the scriptures the following points concerning the character of God:

> First, that he was God before the world was created, and the same God that he was after it was created.
> Secondly, that he is merciful and gracious, slow to anger, abundant in goodness, and that he was so from everlasting, and will be to everlasting.
> Thirdly, that he changes not, neither is there variableness with him; but that he is the same from everlasting to everlasting, being the same yesterday, today, and forever; and that his course is one eternal round, without variation.
> Fourthly, that he is a God of truth and cannot lie.
> Fifthly, that he is no respecter of persons: but in every nation he that fears God and works righteousness is accepted of him.
> Sixthly, that he is love. (*Lectures on Faith* 3:13-18.)

Attributes and Perfections of God

The *Lectures on Faith* also speak of six specific attributes of God, and they are all related:

> We have, in the revelations which [God] has given to the human family, the following account of his attributes:
> First—*Knowledge* . . .
> Secondly—*Faith or power* . . .

39

Some people think that the Lord does not operate by faith because he has all knowledge. In a sense this is true. However, here Joseph Smith is talking about faith as power. If God ceased to have faith, he would cease to have power. Faith, or power, is an eternal attribute of God.

> Thirdly—*Justice* . . .
> Fourthly—*Judgment* . . .
> Fifthly—*Mercy* . . .
> And Sixthly—*Truth* . . . (*Lectures on Faith* 4:4-10; italics added.)

You may want to relate these six qualities to the characteristics of God mentioned earlier, remembering that *the perfections of God are the refinement of his attributes and characteristics,* and that you can refine these characteristics within yourself so that you can become like him.

I have always loved these words of John:

> Behold, what manner of love the Father hath bestowed upon us, that we should be called the sons of God: therefore the world knoweth us not, because it knew him not.
>
> Beloved, now are we the sons of God, and it doth not yet appear what we shall be: but we know that, when he shall appear, *we shall be like him; for we shall see him as he is.*
>
> And every man that hath this hope in him purifieth himself, even as he is pure. (1 John 3:1-3; italics added.)

This teaches us that not only will we see God as he is and know that we are physically in his image (I used to think that was all it meant when I was younger), but it also teaches that if we can continue perfecting and sanctifying ourselves, we can become as he is spiritually.

Jesus said, "This is life eternal, that they might know thee the only true God, and Jesus Christ, whom thou hast sent." (John 17:3.) This, to me, is saying that our eternal life depends upon our coming to know God and what he is really like.

3. Knowledge That Our Course of Life Is According to God's Will

An excellent example of the third element of faith mentioned in the *Lectures* is found in the story of Nephi, for Nephi knew that his course was in accordance with God's will. Let's analyze this story to see if we can determine at least partially how a person knows whether or not he is pursuing the course in life the Lord would have him pursue.

> It came to pass that I, Nephi, returned from speaking with the Lord, to the tent of my father. (1 Nephi 3:1.)

Nephi had been out praying. That is a good place to start in order to know the will of the Lord. Then he went to speak with his father, Lehi.

> And it came to pass that he spake unto me, saying: Behold I have dreamed a dream, in the which the Lord hath commanded me that thou and thy brethren shall return to Jerusalem.
>
> For behold, Laban hath the record of the Jews and also a genealogy of thy forefathers, and they are engraven upon plates of brass. (Verses 2-3.)

At this point we see only two men, a father and a son. There were no angels, no manifestations, and no physical evidences except that a father had said to his son, "I dreamed that you and your brothers should go back to Jerusalem." At that point Nephi had to decide whether to follow the inclinations of the natural man or the spiritual man, whether to doubt or to believe.

> Wherefore, the Lord hath commanded me that thou and thy brothers should go unto the house of Laban, and seek the records, and bring them down hither into the wilderness.
>
> And now, behold thy brothers murmur, saying it is a hard thing which I have required of them; but behold I have not required it of them, but it is a commandment of the Lord. (Verses 4-5.)

Now right here think about yourself and your spiritual condition. What would you have done? Laman and Lemuel murmured, possibly saying such things as "Our father has always been a visionary man. He always has dreams. He could have had a late supper that caused his dream." You can imagine the things they might have said to criticize their father. In effect, they refused to believe the revealed will of the Lord.

Next, consider Nephi. He was in the same situation and heard the same words from his father, but what was his attitude?

> Therefore go, my son, and thou shalt be favored of the Lord, *because thou hast not murmured.* (Verse 6; italics added.)

Nephi heard the same thing, but he believed and did not criticize his father.

> And it came to pass that I, Nephi, said unto my father: *I will go and do* the things which the Lord hath commanded, for I know that the Lord giveth no commandments unto the children of men, save he shall prepare a way for them that they may accomplish the thing which he commandeth them. (Verse 7; italics added.)

Can you see how Nephi put this matter in the proper perspective? It was not Lehi asking him to go to Jerusalem, it was the Lord asking him through Lehi. There is a great difference, and Nephi recognized that.

> And it came to pass that when my father had heard these words he was exceeding glad, for he knew that I had been blessed of the Lord. (Verse 8.)

Theirs was a totally united relationship, and Lehi knew that his son had been blessed by the Lord. Nephi now knew spiritually the truth of his father's words. He knew the Lord's will. All that was left was for him to go and do it.

> And I, Nephi, and my brethren took our journey in the wilderness, with our tents, to go up to the land of Jerusalem. (Verse 9.)

A verse like that is easy to skip over. But can you imagine yourself in that position? It was a long way back to Jerusalem, and I suspect that there were many problems on the way. I don't think the Lord told Nephi where to pitch his tent every night. I doubt that an angel pitched it for him. Nephi did it. He probably did not have a drink of water some nights, or maybe he had trouble getting food. We do not really know the background of that one little verse, but the trip must not have been easy, and the Lord did not do all the work. Nephi did it. It is the same for us today.

> And it came to pass that when we had come up to the land of Jerusalem, I and my brethren did consult one with another. (Verse 10.)

It has always been interesting to me that they counseled together, perhaps asking, "What are we going to do? How are we going to get the plates?" From what they had been told up to that point, it sounded like a fairly easy task. The inclination of the natural man might have been to think, "If the Lord is preparing the way, Laban probably had the same dream our father had. He probably has those plates in a sack waiting for us. All we will have to do is knock on his door and ask for them." These young men could have had every reason to believe that, couldn't they?

They may have come up with a number of alternatives. Perhaps they thought of something like this: "Maybe I can work for Laban a few months in order to win the hand of his daughter and then he will let me have the plates." That is a possibility isn't it? That short verse saying they consulted together tells me that they did not have an easy step-by-step plan for getting the plates from Laban. All they had is what you now have regarding your life, and that is the word of the Lord through his servant. They were told by the Lord to get the plates. They were not told specifically how to get them, but only that they were to obtain them. So they consulted together.

> And we cast lots—who of us should go in unto the house of Laban. And it came to pass that the lot fell upon Laman; and Laman went in unto the house of Laban, and he talked with him as he sat in his house. (Verse 11.)

I suspect again that Laman (as anyone following the inclinations of the natural man) was probably thinking that it would be fairly easy to ask Laban for the plates and receive them.

> And he desired of Laban the records which were engraven upon the plates of brass, which contained the genealogy of my father.
> And behold, it came to pass that Laban was angry, and thrust him out from his presence; and he would not that he should have the records. Wherefore, he said unto him: Behold thou art a robber, and I will slay thee.
> But Laman fled out of his presence, and told the things which Laban had done, unto us. (Verses 12-14.)

I suspect that the brothers were a bit surprised. They had done just as they were told to do in attempting to acquire the plates, but instead of accomplishing their task they had just about lost their lives. It is interesting that Nephi next writes:

> And *we* began to be exceeding sorrowful, . . .

I imagine that they were a bit discouraged, just the way we all are when we set a goal and then fail to reach it.

> . . . and my brethren were about to return unto my father in the wilderness. (Verse 14; italics added.)

Redouble Your Faith in the Lord when Adversity Comes

Laman and Lemuel were quitters. After just one setback they were ready to give up. They probably continued murmuring and criticized Nephi much as they had criticized their father.

Now, think carefully about what happened to Nephi and his brothers, because it relates to you. They had a serious setback. They had tried, with their faith, the best they knew how. Would they ever have gone to the house of Laban if they had not had faith that they would obtain the plates? No, they believed they would or they would not have gone. But their attempt was a failure. They had come to the moment of tribulation, a moment almost every one of us faces every day. They needed to make a decision. Would they go on believing in the Lord's word with double the faith they had before, or would they quit? Laman and Lemuel wanted to go back to the tent of their father. But listen to Nephi, who was filled with great faith.

> But behold I said unto them that: As the Lord liveth, and as we live, we will not go down unto our father in the wilderness until we have accomplished the thing which the Lord hath commanded us. (Verse 15.)

That is strong. Nephi was saying in essence that the Lord lived, and that as surely as He lived and they themselves lived, they would not return until they had accomplished what they had been sent to do. At that particular moment did Nephi have any more knowledge than he had had before in the sense that the task was going to be easy or even that he knew what he was going to do? I do not think so; he was still working with faith. Did he know how he was going to get the plates? No, but he believed he would. He believed so strongly that I feel he understood the great principle that is intertwined throughout this whole experience: When tribulations and problems come, you cannot let your faith weaken, but you must redouble your faith in the Lord. It was situations like this one that Joseph Smith was referring to when he said that when the Lord sees that you are willing to serve him at any price, at any cost, or under any circumstance, then you will have sufficient faith to lay hold upon eternal life, and not until. Nephi was going through that process.

Nephi continued:

> Wherefore, let us be faithful in keeping the commandments of the Lord; therefore let us go down to the land of our father's inheritance, for behold he left gold and silver, and all manner of riches. And all this he hath done because of the commandments of the Lord. (Verse 16.)

In verses 17 through 20 we see Nephi continue to reason with his brothers and stress the importance of their mission as well as the importance of the plates. Then Nephi wrote:

> And it came to pass that after this manner of language did I persuade my brethren, that they might be faithful in keeping the commandments of God. (Verse 21.)

Nephi persuaded them to return and try again to obtain the plates. He hit upon the idea of buying the plates from Laban, and he may have said something like this to his brothers: "If we give Laban all of our riches, surely he will give us the plates." I imagine that Nephi gave his brothers a talk that persuaded them that this time they would be successful. Was Nephi exercising his faith in this plan? Certainly he was, or he never would have done it. However, once again his faith in the specific method was to fail, even though his faith in the Lord's will (that they get the plates) would eventually bear fruit.

> And it came to pass that we went down to the land of our inheritance, and we did gather together our gold, and our silver, and our precious things.
>
> And after we had gathered these things together, we went up again unto the house of Laban.
>
> And it came to pass that we went in unto Laban, and desired him that he would give unto us the records which were engraven upon the plates of brass, for which we would give unto him our gold, and our silver, and all our precious things. (Verses 22-24.)

Was Laban impressed? He seemed to be impressed with the gold but not with giving away the plates.

> And it came to pass that when Laban saw our property, and that it was exceeding great, he did lust after it, insomuch that he thrust us out, and sent his servants to slay us, that he might obtain our property.
>
> And it came to pass that we did flee before the servants of Laban, and we were obliged to leave behind our property, and it fell into the hands of Laban.
>
> And it came to pass that we fled into the wilderness, and the servants of Laban did not overtake us, and we hid ourselves in the cavity of a rock. (Verses 25-27.)

Now the brothers had twice failed to obtain their objective. I wonder how strong our faith would be if we were in the same situation. Twice they had been obedient and had gone up to the house of Laban to acquire the plates. They had lost nearly everything and were now hiding to save their lives. But Nephi, knowing that it was God's will that they succeed, continued to believe.

Know the Timetable of the Lord

> And it came to pass that Laman was angry with me, and also with my father; and also was Lemuel, for *he hearkened unto the words of Laman*. [Notice that one can consistently follow evil as well as good.] Wherefore Laman and Lemuel did speak many hard words unto us, their younger brothers, and they did smite us even with a rod.
>
> And it came to pass as they smote us with a rod, behold, an angel of the Lord came and stood before them, and he spake unto them, saying: Why do ye smite your younger brother with a rod? Know ye not that the Lord hath chosen him to be a ruler over you, and this because of your iniquities? Behold ye shall go up to Jerusalem again, and the Lord will deliver Laban into your hands. (Verses 28-29; italics added.)

There are two important points here that we need to remember. First, after two failures, Nephi still remained strong in the faith. Even when Laman and Lemuel were beating him, he believed. I ask, do *you* still believe when you are being beaten by life? Do you say to the Lord, "I do not know how I am going to do it, Father, but with thy help I am still going to accomplish thy will." Or, do you follow the example of Laman and Lemuel who doubted, murmured, feared, and gave up?

The second point is that Nephi, after resisting two great failures, finally had his faith rewarded. An angel came! Nephi must have needed some support right then, and I imagine that helped. But what did he know, at that moment that he did not know before? The angel said, "Behold ye shall go up to Jerusalem again, and the Lord will deliver Laban into your hands." (Verse 29.) Then Nephi knew the Lord's timetable, which is a very important thing to know. There are many things that are the will of the Lord but whose timetables are not known to man. Keep that in mind when you are trying to accomplish the Lord's will.

> And after the angel had spoken unto us, he departed.
>
> And after the angel had departed, Laman and Lemuel again began to murmur. (Verses 30-31.)

You can see here the impact an angel might have on the faith of an unbeliever—practically none. Laman and Lemuel were "natural men," and after the angel left they asked a "natural-man" question. The Lord does allow us to ask this question, but we must ask it with a faithful attitude. Laman and Lemuel doubtingly asked, "How?": "How is it possible that the Lord will deliver Laban into our hands?" (Verse 31.) Nephi did not know the answer. All he knew was that they were going to go and do it and that *the Lord would provide.* But all Laman and Lemuel could think about was the difficulty of the task.

What they were looking for was a detailed plan for doing the Lord's will, perhaps something like this: (1) Arrive in Jerusalem at 4:00 P.M. (2) Do not enter through the gate: instead, climb over the back wall. (3) Go down Almeida Street. (4) Continue four blocks and then turn to the right. And so on. That may seem kind of silly, perhaps, but in essence that is what they were waiting for before they would believe. With evidence like that almost anyone would believe, but the Lord does not operate that way. The Lord reveals his will *generally* to allow us to have faith in him and to see if we are willing to prove that faith through our own actions, even when we don't understand specifically how to do his will. He reveals light and expects us to walk to the edge of the light or even into the darkness a bit, and only then will he reveal more light and truth.

This reminds me strongly of some great words in the book of Abraham. Abraham was shown the intelligences that were organized before the world was and he was told that he himself was one of them. Then he was taught one of the great purposes of this life:

> There stood one among them that was like unto God, and he said unto those who were with him: We will go down, for there is space there, and we will take of these materials, and we will make an earth whereon these may dwell;
>
> *And we will prove them herewith, to see if they will do all things whatsoever the Lord their God shall command them.* (Abraham 3:24-25; italics added.)

The Lord gives us his commandments through the scriptures, the prophets, and the promptings of the Holy Spirit, but he expects us to work out, through our faith, the specific ways to keep his commandments. How could we ever become like him if he made every decision for us, if he held our hand every step of the way?

The Specifics of How to Accomplish the Lord's Will Are Mostly Unknown

Let's return to Nephi, who was right in the midst of proving his faith. Laman and Lemuel continued to murmur, saying:

> How is it possible that the Lord will deliver Laban into our hands? Behold, he is a mighty man, and he can command fifty, yea, even he can slay fifty; then why not us? (Verse 31.)

Laman and Lemuel were impressed with the power of the world. I imagine as they escaped for the second time, they had actually seen the swords and realized they had barely escaped alive. Try to imagine this situation as Laman and Lemuel saw it. They had seen an angel and then had to compare this with fifty men with swords. In the mind of a natural man, the comparison might go something like this: "I saw an angel, didn't I? I am pretty sure of it, but one thing I know for sure, and this is that I saw fifty men with swords." Nephi had to make the same comparison, but when he was confronted with the arguments of his brothers, he gave them an answer that was full of faith:

> Let us go up again unto Jerusalem, and let us be faithful in keeping the commandments of the Lord; . . .

Notice that almost every time Nephi spoke, he mentioned the commandments of the Lord. He was not saying, "Let's go do what our father said to do." He was saying, "Let's go do what the Lord said to do." Now I am sure the Lord appreciates it when you bear your testimony that he lives. But what really counts is your love for the Lord and whether you do his will and keep his commandments. Listen to Nephi's reasoning and you will learn the strength of his faith in the Lord:

> . . . for behold he is mightier than all the earth, then why not mightier than Laban and his fifty, yea, or even than his tens of thousands. (1 Nephi 4:1.)

I would suggest that when you have the same attitude in the midst of tribulations, you will eventually see your faith rewarded.

> Therefore let us go up; let us be strong like unto Moses; for he truly spake unto the waters of the Red Sea and they divided hither and thither, and our fathers came through, out of captivity, on dry ground, and the armies of Pharaoh did follow and were drowned in the waters of the Red Sea.
>
> Now behold ye know that this is true; and ye also know that an angel hath spoken unto you; wherefore can ye doubt? Let us go up; and the Lord is able to deliver us, even as our fathers, and to destroy Laban, even as the Egyptians.

Nephi taught his brothers that the Lord would deal with them the same way that he did with Moses. The Lord will deal with you today the same way.

The Lord Allows Latitude for Human Judgment

Then Nephi wrote:

> Now when I had spoken these words, they were yet wroth, and did still continue to murmur; nevertheless they did follow me up until we came without the walls of Jerusalem.
>
> And it was by night; and I caused that they should hide themselves without the walls. (Verses 4-5.)

If Nephi had known in advance exactly what was going to happen, if he had known that they would have been protected and that all would have gone well, would he have left his brothers outside the walls to hide themselves? I doubt it. But he did, because he did not know what was going to happen—he took that extra precaution. The Lord was allowing him to take that judgment upon himself, which allowed him to grow.

> And after they had hid themselves, I, Nephi, crept into the city and went forth towards the house of Laban. (Verse 5.)

We find the capstone to all that we have been talking about in the next verse:

> And I was led by the Spirit, not knowing beforehand the things I should do. Nevertheless I went forth. (Verses 6-7.)

Nephi went forth determined to do the Lord's will, even though he did not know exactly how to do it. Right after that, the Lord began to reveal to Nephi almost exactly what should be done. And, finally, he was able to obtain the plates. But this did not happen until *after* the trial of his faith. *It was not until the Lord knew that Nephi would serve him at any cost that he revealed to him his specific will.* Then he allowed Nephi to have his Spirit to bless him and instruct him.

You are in the same position as Nephi was. As you go forward in faith, the Lord will reveal his will to you so that you will know what you should do. I have been greatly moved to see the amount of revelation that the Lord has poured out upon the members of his church about how to do his work and solve their problems, just as Nephi had revelation poured out upon him. When you sincerely say to the Lord, "Father, I believe thy will, and I will do it; I will give all that it takes to accomplish it," and then you keep that promise, the Lord will reveal to you how to do it. Then you will know that the course of your life is according to his will, and you will be able to exercise your faith in him, not just to keep his commandments, but to obtain life and salvation.

Questions to Ponder

1. On what should we base our faith?

_____

_____

_____

2. What three things do the *Lectures on Faith* say are necessary to exercise faith in God unto life and salvation?

_____

_____

_____

3. In what ways do we learn about the existence of God?

_____

_____

_____

4. Why does God want us to know of his existence?

_____

_____

_____

5. In what ways can we learn of God's attributes?

_____

_____

_____

6. How does knowing about God's attributes help us have faith in him?

_____

_____

_____

7. What are some of the attributes and characteristics of God?

_____

_____

_____

8. How can we know that our course of life is according to God's will?

_____

_____

_____

9. Reread the story of Nephi related in this chapter. What principles can you learn from this story that will help you solve any problems you are currently having?

_____

_____

_____

Chapter Five

Obtaining Faith

A few years ago I visited the famous ancient Incan ruins, Machu Picchu, near Cuzco, Peru. Before returning to Cuzco, up on the mountain, I met a man who I learned was a rather learned archaeologist. He was enthralled with the ruins; it was the first time he'd ever been to Machu Picchu, although he'd been to many other ruins. He named sites I'd never even heard of, and I thought I'd been to quite a few. He'd been to ruins of ruins. We talked a little bit about Machu Picchu, and then I led him into a gospel discussion. I asked, "Who were these people, and what were they doing here?" But as soon as I mentioned the Book of Mormon, he immediately hardened his heart. He said, "I don't want to hear from you, Mr. Cook, about church or religion." A straightforward rejection like that is a challenge that has to be met by approaching the subject from a different angle. So I said to him, "I know you're a scientist, so I won't talk to you about spiritual ways of knowing the truth. But I'd like you to answer just two or three questions for me." And then I said to myself, "What questions, Brother Cook? I hope the Spirit comes through, because these two or three questions I'm going to ask this man, what are they?" And one of them was this: "The book *Gone With the Wind* is full of historical errors—anachronisms. It took the author about ten years to write it. How do you explain the fact that Joseph Smith translated the Book of Mormon in just sixty days?" Then I was quiet and just listened. "Well," he said, "I don't know. I'd have to assume first of all that that's true." And I said, "It is, it's documented in history." And he said, "Well, I don't know the answer." So I said, "Well, let's try this one. You know as well as I do that ten or fifteen years ago, archaeologists said that cement had been discovered only in Europe, and that copper was not known to the ancient Americans. When Joseph Smith published the Book of Mormon saying there were cement roads, copper implements, horses, and elephants in the Americas, the world laughed. Today, as you know, archaeologists have found all those things on this continent. I've walked on cement roads, and I've seen hundreds of copper knives and the bones of horses and elephants. Cortez brought horses with him, true, but horses were here a long time before Cortez. Now, how did Joseph Smith know to put those things in the Book of Mormon in the year 1830?" What could this man say?

And, as Alma said to Korihor, I said to this man, "You have no evidence save your word only that there is no God." (See Alma 30:40.) Do you see how powerful that is? Then the man began to retreat, because I had really put the pressure on him. But he retreated only as far as an agnostic usually does. He said, "Well, Mr. Cook, I won't say whether there is a God or not; I don't know." Do you see where he was? He was still right on the neutral line. And that doesn't serve for anything. A person has to get off the line. He has to have at least a desire to believe. If he'll only do that he can begin to obtain faith. But if he won't, he won't get anywhere.

In analyzing how to obtain faith, we should study the principles that we can learn from the scriptures. Some of these principles are discussed under the following six subheadings. As you read these six sections, please continually refer to the diagram on page 63.

1. Desire to Believe

Alma explained the way to obtain faith:

> Now, as I said, concerning faith—that it was not a perfect knowledge—even so it is with my words. Ye cannot know of their

surety at first, unto perfection, any more than faith is a perfect knowledge.

But behold, if ye will awake and arouse your faculties, even to an experiment upon my words, and exercise a particle of faith, yea, *even if ye can no more than desire to believe,* let this desire work in you, even until ye believe in a manner that ye can give place for a portion of my words. (Alma 32:26-27; italics added.)

The Lord does not expect someone, in the beginning, to believe with no evidence. Later on he might, but in the beginning he provides evidence. He gave the greatest evidence of all that he existed by appearing to Joseph Smith. And we have great evidence in the Book of Mormon—there are evidences by the thousands. We have the testimonies of the prophets and of others. And we have the promptings of the Holy Spirit. As you grow spiritually, you will require less and less evidence in order to believe, but in the beginning, you need some evidence. But even with evidence, you must have a desire to believe. Without that desire, you would not believe even great evidence. But with it, you have begun the process of acquiring faith, and the Holy Ghost will help you reach the point where you can believe a portion of the Lord's word.

2. Believe on the Lord's Word

Now, we will compare the word unto a seed. Now, if ye give place, that a seed may be planted in your heart, behold, if it be a true seed, or a good seed, if ye do not cast it out by your unbelief, that ye will resist the Spirit of the Lord, behold, it will begin to swell within your breasts.

If you give place that a good seed (a portion of the Lord's word) may be planted in your heart, you must be careful not to cast it out by your unbelief. This does not just apply to gaining a testimony; it is true of exercising your faith as a father, a mother, a priesthood leader, or a missionary, or in any aspect of life. Every day we cast out great things because of our unbelief. But if we do not cast out that portion of the Lord's word in our hearts, it will begin to grow within us, to swell within our breasts. I think this is Alma's way of describing the burning in the bosom, or the witness of the Spirit to the truthfulness of the Lord's word.

And when you feel these swelling motions, ye will begin to say within yourselves—it must needs be that this is a good seed, or that the word is good, for [1] it beginneth to enlarge my soul; [2] yea it beginneth to enlighten my understanding, [3] yea, it beginneth to be delicious to me. (Verse 28.)

3. Experiment and Obtain Spiritual Evidences

At that point you are dealing with evidence—you know that you feel something, for you have felt these "swelling motions." But Alma, by inspiration, did not end his explanation there, and I'm thankful for that, because different people may have different ideas about what that spiritual feeling is and what it means. So how do you correctly recognize that feeling and know that the seed (the word) is from God? Alma gives three definite evidences that tell you if the seed comes from the Lord:

1. It begins to enlarge your soul.
2. It begins to enlighten your understanding.
3. It begins to be delicious to you.

Several years ago, some stake missionaries were teaching a man in our ward who understood the gospel but for some reason would not join the Church. One of the missionaries came to me and said, "Elder Cook, I'm sure if you visited this man with us, we could persuade him to be baptized." I was rusty; I had been off my mission for a number of years. What could I do? You see, I had some unbelief in my heart. But he expressed faith in me, saying again, "Elder Cook, I am sure that if you go to that man you can persuade him to be baptized." He had faith that the Lord could work through us to help this man join the Church, so what could I say? We prayed that the will of the Lord might be done, and then we went to visit the man. He had had the missionary lessons so many times he probably knew them better than I did. I learned the first fifteen minutes of our discussion that he wasn't avoiding baptism because of lack of knowledge or understanding. I also found out that he was obeying the commandments. So we quickly got down to the heart of the problem. The man said, "Elder Cook, I guess I just don't really know that the Church is true. If I knew it was true, I would join, but I don't really know."

Now, I had already felt that he knew, but that he didn't *know* that he knew. I said to him, "Brother, I would like you to do something for me. I want you to take this sheet of paper and write down all the reasons you can think of why you shouldn't be baptized. We'll help you dream them up." The man's wife, who was a member of the Church, was sitting there, so I said to her, too, "You help us. Let's try to think of every conceivable reason why your husband should not be baptized."

The man tried to think of some reasons, but the only one he could come up with was that he wasn't sure the Church was true. He could have said, "It would be hard for me to discipline myself to this life," but he had already been doing that. So I said to him, "If we could help you resolve this one reason, would you be baptized?" And he said he would. So he had committed himself. Then I felt the words of the Lord come into my mind, and I said to him, "Brother, would you tell us a few experiences you have had with the missionaries when you've felt that your soul has been enlarged?" I'd never said those words before. They just came out. He said, "Well, when these elders first started coming here, I used to swear. Oh, how I used to swear! I was terrible. But I feel that my soul has been enlarged because they taught me not to swear, and I haven't sworn since." Then he told us a few more examples of how his soul had been enlarged, and I said, "Now tell us about some times when you've felt that your mind has been enlightened, would you?" Of course, we were writing his answers down as he went. And he told us about when his mind was enlightened: "You know, I had had a problem that worried me all this time, and the elders came and taught me, and it just disappeared." Then the words came to me again and I said, "Does the gospel seem kind of delicious to you? Do you enjoy it? Does it just kind of taste good?" "Well, yes, it really does," he said. Then he told us a few experiences to show that it was delicious to him. And only then did I remember the passage on faith in Alma 32. I didn't even know what it said in there for sure—roughly, but not word for word. I opened the Book of Mormon to that passage and said, "Let's read," and we started reading, and when we came to those three tests of truth, that good brother not only knew that the gospel was true, but he *knew* that he knew. On the following Saturday he was baptized a member of The Church of Jesus Christ of Latter-day Saints.

I tell you that story to show you a little bit about how to obtain faith in the Lord's word. Whether that word comes through the scriptures, your bishop, your stake president, or the Prophet, the process is the same. For example, President Kimball has asked us to hold Family Home Evening—we have received the Lord's word. If we experiment upon that word, doing what the Prophet has asked, we will receive the three evidences spoken of by Alma that President Kimball's request is from the Lord. And, as Alma says, "Would not this increase your faith?" (Alma 32:29.) Of course it would.

4. Your Faith Is Strengthened and Increased

Alma continues:

> I say unto you, Yea, nevertheless, it hath not grown up to a perfect knowledge.
>
> But behold, as the seed swelleth, and sprouteth, and beginneth to grow, then you must needs say that the seed is good; for behold it swelleth, and sprouteth, and beginneth to grow.
>
> And now, behold, will this not strengthen your faith? Yea, it will strengthen your faith: for ye will say I know that this is a good seed: for behold it sprouteth and beginneth to grow.
>
> And now, behold, are ye sure that this is a good seed? I say unto you, Yea; for every seed bringeth forth unto its own likeness.
>
> Therefore, if a seed groweth it is good, but if it groweth not, behold it is not good, therefore it is cast away.
>
> And now, behold, because ye have tried the experiment, and planted the seed, and it swelleth and sprouteth, and beginneth to grow, ye must needs know that the seed is good.

5. You Obtain a Perfect Knowledge in That Thing

> And now, behold, is your knowledge perfect? Yea, your knowledge is perfect in that thing, and your faith is dormant; and this

because you know, for ye know that the word hath swelled your souls, and ye also know that it hath sprouted up, that your understanding doth begin to be enlightened, and your mind doth begin to expand.

O then, is not this real? I say unto you, Yea, because it is light; and whatsoever is light, is good, because it is discernible, therefore ye must know that it is good. (Verses 29-35.)

6. Nourish the Word

After you have obtained this faith and this knowledge, you must not stop, but you must continue nourishing the word until you can obtain eternal life. Alma continues:

And now behold, after ye have tasted this light is your knowledge perfect?

Behold I say unto you, Nay; neither must ye lay aside your faith, for ye have only exercised your faith to plant the seed that ye might try the experiment to know if the seed was good.

And behold, as the tree beginneth to grow, ye will say: Let us nourish it with great care, that it may get root, that it may grow up, and bring forth fruit unto us. And now behold, if ye nourish it with much care it will get root, and grow up, and bring forth fruit.

But if ye neglect the tree, and take no thought for its nourishment, behold it will not get any root; and when the heat of the sun cometh and scorcheth it, because it hath no root it withers away, and ye pluck it up and cast it out.

Now, this is not because the seed was not good, neither is it because the fruit thereof would not be desirable; but it is because your ground is barren, and ye will not nourish the tree, therefore ye cannot have the fruit thereof.

And thus, if ye will not nourish the word, looking forward with an eye of faith to the fruit thereof, ye can never pluck of the fruit of the tree of life.

But if ye will nourish the word, yea, nourish the tree as it beginneth to grow, by your faith with great diligence, and with patience, looking forward to the fruit thereof, it shall take root; and behold it shall be a tree springing up unto everlasting life.

And because of your diligence and your faith and your patience with the word in nourishing it, that it may take root in you, behold, by and by ye shall pluck the fruit thereof, which is most precious, which is sweet above all that is sweet, and which is white above all that is white, yea, and pure above all that is pure; and ye shall feast upon this fruit even until ye are filled, that ye hunger not, neither shall ye thirst.

Then, my brethren, ye shall reap the rewards of your faith, and your diligence, and patience, and long-suffering, waiting for the tree to bring forth fruit unto you. (Verses 35-43.)

At this point in obtaining faith, you have been through a very important process. You have heard the word of the Lord. You have desired to believe. You have experimented upon the word. And, finally, you have obtained not only faith in the word, but a knowledge of it and how to nourish it. (See the diagram on the next page.) But there are a few other factors to keep in mind in the process of obtaining faith.

In addition to the six elements just described, you must keep in mind that faith is a gift of God, that you must center your faith in Jesus Christ, that you must use the power of the Holy Ghost, and that you must recognize and be thankful for the faith you already have.

Faith Is a Gift of God

Faith truly is a gift of God. And we may obtain this gift from God by seeking after it. Moroni wrote:

> To one is given by the Spirit of God, that he may teach the word of wisdom;
>
> And to another, that he may teach the word of knowledge by the same Spirit;
>
> And to another, *exceedingly great faith;* . . . and all these gifts come by the Spirit of Christ; and they come unto every man severally, according as he will. (Moroni 10:9-11, 17; italics added.)

We learn from Moroni that one way to obtain faith is to seek for this gift from the Lord. That suggests to me that if you really want to have more faith, you would be wise to pray with all of your heart to obtain it and then be willing to receive what the Lord will give you in order for you to have more faith. We should not expect faith to drop from heaven and descend upon us. It does not typ-

The Process for Believing the Lord's Word

(See Alma 32)

1 Desire to believe	2 Believe on the words	3 Experiment and obtain spiritual evidences	4 Faith is strengthened and increased	5 Perfect knowledge is obtained in that thing	6 Nourish the word
Forces of Unbelief - - - - - - -		- - - - - Tribulation - - - - -		- - - - - Intense Opposition	
The minds of men are so constructed that they will not believe, without a testimony of seeing or hearing." (Oliver Cowdery.)	A person must believe beyond where he is. He must commit to pay any price to know.	These evidences—it beginneth to enlarge my soul; it beginneth to enlighten my understanding; it beginneth to be delicious—cause faith to grow, and allow a person to know from his own experience good from evil.	A person must observe his covenants by sacrifice. He has seen his faith rewarded before, and is certain it will happen again.	A person knows by his experience that a thing is true.	"...by your faith with great diligence, and with patience ... springing up unto everlasting life." (Alma 32:41.)

ically come that way. Faith comes as the Lord provides us with experiences and challenges that will strengthen us as we live righteously. Faith comes by a lot of hard work, a lot of patience, and a lot of time. Remember as you pray for the gift of faith, that you must prepare yourself to receive whatever the Lord may send you.

Center Your Faith in the Lord Jesus Christ

Where we center our faith is another essential principle that has to do with faith and how we obtain it. We must center our faith in the Lord Jesus Christ in the way he has prescribed. Nephi wrote:

> We talk of Christ, we rejoice in Christ, we preach of Christ, we prophesy of Christ, and we write according to our prophecies, that our children may know to what source they may look for a remission of their sins . . .
>
> And now behold, I say unto you that the right way is to believe in Christ, and deny him not; and Christ is the Holy One of Israel; wherefore ye must bow down before him, and worship him with all your might, mind, and strength, and your whole soul; and if ye do this ye shall in nowise be cast out. (2 Nephi 25:26, 29.)

I remember an interview I once had with a young man who had broken the law of chastity as a serviceman in Japan. In the process of bringing things to light and clearing everything up, I asked why he did it. His answer was interesting and a direct contrast to the counsel of the scriptures. He said, "The reason I kept the law of chastity all of my life up until now was because of my mother. I could never have done anything to offend her and her beauty and her purity. I kept the law of chastity because of her. And then when I was eight thousand miles away and she was nowhere near, my faith faltered because it was centered in an erroneous idea to begin with. And thus I fell." As I heard those words, I knew that I could *never* afford to center my faith in anything or anyone other than the Lord Jesus Christ. He is the rock of our salvation. He is immovable. His course is one eternal round, and you can depend on him wherever you are throughout your life and throughout all eternity. He will always be the same.

The prophet Alma asked a series of penetrating questions that we would do well to think about:

> And now behold, I ask of you, my brethren of the church, have ye spiritually been born of God? Have ye received his image in your countenances? Have ye experienced this mighty change in your hearts?
>
> Do ye exercise faith in the redemption of him who created you? Do you look forward with an eye of faith, and view this mortal body raised in immortality, and this corruption raised in incorruption, to stand before God to be judged according to the deeds which have been done in the mortal body? (Alma 5:14-15.)

Alma taught us that we must center all on the Lord. Through the Lord, we must have hope, and through him we must look forward to the time of the resurrection of our bodies. For, as Mormon said, "In Christ there should come every good thing." (Moroni 7:22.)

Use the Power of the Holy Ghost

The power of the Holy Ghost is another key element in obtaining faith. The Holy Ghost is the revelator of all things, including the attributes of God upon which faith is based. The truths that you will obtain spiritually as a member of the Church will come through the Holy Ghost. The Lord told Adam:

> It is given to abide in you; the record of heaven; the Comforter; the peaceable things of immortal glory; the truth of all things; that which quickeneth all things, which maketh alive all things; that which knoweth all things, and hath all power according to wisdom, mercy, truth, justice, and judgment. (Moses 6:61.)

This verse names some of the attributes of God that are revealed by the Holy Ghost so that we can obtain faith in God.

Elder Bruce R. McConkie wrote:

> *Faith is based on truth, and is preceded by knowledge. Until a person gains a knowledge of the truth he can have no faith ... Faith and truth cannot be separated; if there is to be faith, saving faith, faith unto life and salvation, faith that leads to the celestial world,*

there must first be truth. Not only is a true knowledge of God a conditioned precedent to the acquirement of this faith, but *faith can be exercised only by those who conform to the principles of truth which come from the true God who actually exists.* (Mormon Doctrine [Salt Lake City: Bookcraft, 1966], p. 262.)

What Elder McConkie is saying, as I understand it, is that faith is based on truth. If a person has a false concept of what God is, he might still by his faith or belief bring about some changes in his life. He can certainly receive answers to his prayers. However, he does not have a saving faith, a faith that will place him in the celestial kingdom. The only way that kind of faith can be exercised is if it is based on a *true knowledge of God,* and no other way. And a true knowledge of God comes through the ministrations of the Holy Ghost.

The *Lectures on Faith* state:

> How do men obtain a knowledge of the glory of God, his perfections and attributes? By devoting themselves to his service, through prayer and supplication incessantly strengthening their faith in him, until, like Enoch, the brother of Jared, and Moses, they obtain a manifestation of God to themselves. (*Lectures on Faith*, from questions and answers following lecuure 2.)

After your service, patience, and incessant prayer, the Lord will reveal himself to you, and you will obtain the kind of faith that you need in order to have eternal life. All such manifestations and revelations come through the Holy Ghost. As you examine your life, are you consciously and diligently working with the Lord's help to be worthy of the companionship of the Holy Ghost?

The *Lectures on Faith* also say:

> After any portion of the human family are made acquainted with the important fact, that there is a God, who has created and does uphold all things, the extent of their knowledge respecting his character and glory will depend upon their diligence and faithfulness in seeking after him, until, like Enoch, the brother of Jared, and Moses, they shall obtain faith in God, and power with him to behold him face to face. (*Lectures on Faith* 2:55.)

This is an open, righteous charge to continue to purify and sanctify ourselves until, by diligently and faithfully seeking after the Lord, we can finally behold him face to face.

Recognize the Faith You Already Have

Do you have faith or do you not have faith? I would suggest that you do have faith or you would not be reading this book. We must be very careful that we do not overly condemn ourselves in thinking we do not have faith. We may have little in comparison to the Lord, but we do have some, at least in an elemental stage.

The Anti-Nephi-Lehies, who were converted by Ammon and Aaron and their brethren, were great Lamanites who were baptized by water and by the Spirit. As the Lord came to visit the inhabitants of the American continent, he said these words about these Lamanites:

> Whoso cometh unto me with a broken heart and a contrite spirit, him will I baptize with fire and with the Holy Ghost, even as the Lamanites, because of their faith in me at the time of their conversion, were baptized with fire and with the Holy Ghost, *and they knew it not.* (3 Nephi 9:20; italics added.)

Isn't that interesting? They were baptized with fire and the Holy Ghost, but they did not know it, possibly because they were still not completely in tune spiritually. So in that same sense I would ask you, do you have faith? Yes, but perhaps you "knew it not." Have you been baptized by fire and by the Holy Ghost? I am sure that in some degree you have, but perhaps you "knew it not." As we become more spiritually sensitive, we begin to realize as we look at ourselves that great things are happening to us spiritually that are not at all perceivable in the natural realm.

When I was younger and questioned certain things because I had not yet received a witness of my own, the words of Moroni held me firm to the gospel, because I could not deny them. He wrote:

And now I come to that faith, of which I said I would speak; and I will tell you the way whereby ye may lay hold on every good thing.

That sounds like something good to know, doesn't it? I would like to know how to lay hold on every good thing.

For behold, God knowing all things, being from everlasting to everlasting, behold, he sent angels to minister unto the children of men, to make manifest concerning the coming of Christ; *and in Christ there should come every good thing.* (Verse 22.)

In other words, everything that is good comes by way of Jesus Christ.

For he hath answered the ends of the law, and *he claimeth all those who have faith in him;* . . .

He will claim you if you have faith in him. If you do not, you will be claimed by someone else by whom you would rather not be claimed.

. . . and *they who have faith in him will cleave unto every good thing;* . . .

Now, that is a great spiritual key.

Wherefore, *all things which are good cometh of God;* and *that which is evil cometh of the devil; for the devil is an enemy unto God, and fighteth against him continually, and inviteth and enticeth to sin, and to do that which is evil continually.*

When I was younger and I examined the principles taught in the Book of Mormon or that I heard taught in the Church, they all led me to do good, all of them. There was nothing that enticed me to do evil. The teachings always had the effect of trying to make me a better person. If something entices me to do good, it must be from the Lord, because all good things come from him.

Mormon continued:

For behold, my brethren, *it is given unto you to judge, that ye may know good from evil;* and the way to judge is as plain, that ye may know with a perfect knowledge, as the daylight is from the dark night.

For behold, *the Spirit of Christ is given to every man, that he may know good from evil; wherefore, I show unto you the way to judge; for every thing which inviteth to do good, and to persuade to believe in Christ, is sent forth by the power and gift of Christ; wherefore ye may know with a perfect knowledge it is of God.*

But whatsoever thing persuadeth men to do evil, and believe not in Christ, and deny him, and serve not God, then ye may know with a perfect knowledge it is of the devil; for after this manner doth the devil work, for he persuadeth no man to do good, no, not one; neither do his angels; neither do they who subject themselves unto him. (Moroni 7:12, 15-17, 22, 28; italics added.)

We need to be careful not to misjudge ourselves. We do have faith in the Lord. Sometimes it is not easy to know how much we have. We struggle many times when we see how much faith other people might have, or how much the Lord has in his perfection, and it makes us feel very humble to realize that we have very little. But we may obtain the faith we desire to have as we continue to pray, to study the scriptures, and to apply the Lord's teachings in our lives.

The Savior said, "Behold, I stand at the door, and knock: if any man hear my voice, and open the door, I will come in to him, and will sup with him, and he with me." (Revelation 3:20.)

Questions to Ponder

1. What is the beginning point for developing faith?

_____

_____

_____

2. How does faith relate to evidence?

_____

_____

_____

3. What three evidences does Alma give that something comes from God?

_____

_____

_____

4. What evidence does Mormon give that something comes from God?

_____

_____

_____

5. What can you do to obtain the gift of faith?

_____

_____

_____

6. Where should you center your faith? What things can you do to do this?

_____

_____

_____

7. How can the Holy Ghost help you obtain faith? What can you do today to bring the Holy Ghost more fully into your life?

_____

_____

_____

Chapter Six

Increasing Faith

In February 1977, while I was president of the Uruguay/ Paraguay Mission, my general authority area supervisor, Elder James E. Faust, came to talk with me and my two counselors. The cornerstone laying of the Sao Paulo temple was scheduled for March 9, just three and a half weeks away, but the Uruguay/Paraguay Mission and stake had gathered only about half of their portion of the temple fund. It had taken a year and a half to raise that much money. Elder Faust said to us, "You know, it would really be a good thing if on the eighth of March you could tell President Kimball that all of the temple funds in your mission had been collected." He didn't tell us to collect the funds. He didn't even ask us to. As general authorities almost always do, he merely gave us a suggestion, hoping that we would hear the voice of the Spirit saying, "Do it."

The first thought that came to my mind was the difficulty of the situation. I knew how many thousands of dollars we were lacking, and I knew that the Uruguayan people didn't have that much money. I remember thinking, "Do you know what you are asking? You are talking about three and a half weeks." And then the Spirit quickly overcame those negative thoughts, and I said, "Elder Faust, we will do it." I asked my counselors if they were in agreement, and they were.

71

Elder Faust left a very happy man that day, but we were left with a big burden. What were we going to do? We prayed about it and determined that Elder Faust's suggestion was the will of the Lord and that we would accept it as such. We talked, and I knew that first of all *we* would have to be committed. I had given money to the fund and my counselors had already given twice. I said to them, "Brethren, do you really believe that we can do this in three weeks? Let's be frank—do you really believe?" And these good men felt the Spirit, and they both said, "We believe." In order to show our faith we each took a piece of paper and wrote down *how much* we believed, in dollars. It was hard on those good brethren to commit again, but it was as one drop of rain on an ocean in terms of fulfilling the whole amount. I knew if we were in tune spiritually as a presidency, that things would move.

After we did that, I said, "Brethren, if you are willing—and you be the judge of whether you are or not—I would like us to commit that one way or another on March 8 that money will be paid, even if it so be that the three of us pay it all." Now the stakes were really high, but I wanted to know how deep our faith ran. Both of these good brethren, without batting an eye, said, "We commit to you and to the Lord that that money will be paid. We have faith in the Saints that they will pay it, but if they don't— we will." Now as those brethren went out to tell district presidents and branch presidents about faith in the Lord and about how to raise the money, they could testify from the depths of their souls that this thing could be brought to pass. As the money began to pour in, we were overjoyed with the response from the Saints, and within about two weeks we had every single dollar and more. It would have been easy to raise the money if we could have collected $5,000 from each of us and $10,000 from each district president. But that would have been impossible, and I knew that some people had given their rings, watches, and, in some cases, even the gold in their teeth to raise the funds that were needed. But because they, and we, were required to stretch and to risk, the faith of all involved was increased, and we were able to raise in two weeks the amount of money it had previously taken us a year and a half to collect.

If you want to increase your faith, you must set up experiences that will cause you to stretch, and you must pray to the Lord with all of your heart that you will be able to accomplish his will in the tasks you have set for yourself. Those are the times when you really grow. Those are the times when you really increase your faith. A missionary who can already memorize five concepts in one hour and sets that as his goal is foolish—he knows he can do it. He should set a goal of ten, a goal that will really cost him something. Then he will say, in the depths of humility, "I have no alternative but to turn to the Lord, because I cannot do this on my own." As long as you try to do only what you already know you can do, you are not going to grow much. You must look beyond where you are and what you are capable of doing to pull down power from heaven to help fulfill it. Then your faith will increase.

In analyzing how to increase our faith, we should listen for the promptings of the Spirit and study the principles of faith outlined in the scriptures. Six of these important principles are discussed under the subheadings throughout the rest of this chapter.

Increasing Your Hope

One way to increase your faith is to increase your ablity to hope, for faith and hope are deeply interrelated. In Ether 12:4 we read:

> Wherefore, whoso believeth in God might with surety hope for a better world, yea, even a place at the right hand of God, *which hope cometh of faith*, maketh an anchor to the souls of men, which would make them sure and steadfast, always abounding in good works, being led to glorify God. (Italics added.)

This suggests that as we exercise our faith, we will have more hope. But the reverse is also true. As Mormon said, "How is it that ye can attain unto faith, save ye shall have hope?" (Moroni 7:40.) You must hope with all your heart for a good cause, that it will come about, and if you exercise your faith in it, and if it be right, it *will* come to pass.

The Apostle Paul wrote:

> We are saved by hope: but hope that is seen is not hope: for what a man seeth, why doth he yet hope for?
>
> But if we hope for that we see not, then do we with patience wait for it. (Romans 8:24-25.)

Paul indicates in these verses that if you see something that already exists, you do not need to hope for it because it already is. What you must do is spiritually perceive something that the world cannot see. You see it spiritually in your mind and then with patience wait for it. Then you have something to hope for. That is what happened during the collection of the temple funds. This miracle was envisioned spiritually, and it gave us something to hope for with all of our hearts. Then we built up our faith and went to work, and the Lord began to accomplish his purposes. But he did not do it until we had first perceived it spiritually.

Hearing the Word of God

Another way to increase your faith is by hearing the word of God. Paul wrote:

> How then shall they [all of us] call on him in whom they have not believed?

In other words, how can we call upon the Lord if we do not even believe in Him yet?

> And how shall they believe in him of whom they have not heard?

We cannot believe in the Lord if we have never heard of him or learned about him.

> And how shall they hear without a preacher?
>
> And how shall they preach, except they be sent? As it is written, How beautiful are the feet of them that preach the gospel of peace, and bring glad tidings of good things! . . .

Paul is talking about priesthood authority here.

> So then *faith cometh by hearing, and hearing by the word of God.* (Romans 10:14-17; italics added.)

That teaches us that one way we can increase our faith is by hearing the word of God. It also teaches us something about being at sacrament meeting and our other meetings where we can hear members of the Church preach the word of God. Any time that we have the opportunity to hear the word of God preached by the Spirit, we have an opportunity to increase our faith. The Lord has said so.

Notice how the words of King Benjamin strengthened the faith of his people:

> When King Benjamin had . . . spoken to his people, he sent among them, desiring to know . . . if they believed the words which he had spoken unto them.
>
> And they all cried with one voice, saying: Yea, we believe all the words which thou hast spoken unto us; and also, we know of their surety and truth, because of the Spirit of the Lord Omnipotent, which has wrought a mighty change in us, or in our hearts, that we have no more disposition to do evil, but to do good continually.
>
> And we, ourselves, also, through the infinite goodness of God, and the manifestations of his Spirit, have great views of that which is to come; and were it expedient, we could prophesy of all things.
>
> And it is the faith which we have had on the things which our king has spoken unto us that has brought us to this great knowledge, whereby we do rejoice with such exeedingly great joy. (Mosiah 5:1-4.)

Reading Prayerfully the Word of God

Closely related to hearing the word of God is reading the word of God, and both will help you increase your faith. Nephi said:

> Hear ye the words of the prophet, *which were written unto all the house of Israel, and liken them unto yourselves, that ye may have hope as well as your brethren.* (1 Nephi 19:24; italics added.)

This indicates that if we will liken the scriptures unto ourselves, they will give us hope. One of the greatest bulwarks in my life has been studying the scriptures and attempting to incorporate them into my life. They have given me a hope that the Lord would provide. I have seen difficult circumstances, when accomplishing what the Lord would have me do seemed impossible. But because I knew what he had done with people in the scriptures, and knowing that he is no respecter of persons, I received the hope and the faith that he would help me in the same way. And he has. And he will help you.

Jacob, the brother of Nephi, said:

> We search the prophets [the scriptures], and we have many revelations and the spirit of prophecy; and having all these witnesses we obtain a hope, and *our faith becometh unshaken*, insomuch that we truly can command in the name of Jesus and the very trees obey us, or the mountains, or the waves of the sea. (Jacob 4:6; italics added.)

That passage tells us that by studying the prophecies and words of the Lord, our hope and faith in the Lord will truly become unshakable.

Acting in Accordance with Present Understanding

Another way to increase your faith is to act in accordance with what you presently understand. In fact, this is a key element in developing faith. You must act according to your present knowledge and understanding of the gospel. In his lecture "True Faith," Orson Pratt states:

> The only way to receive additional faith and light is to practice according to the light which we have: and if we do this, we have the promise of God that the same shall grow brighter and brighter until the perfect day. (In *A Compilation Containing the Lectures on Faith* [Salt Lake City: N.B. Lundwall, n.d.], p. 84.)

This indicates—and I have noticed this in my own life—that if a person receives an understanding of a gospel principle and then lives according to that understanding, correcting his life and putting it in order with respect to that principle, the Lord will immediately bless him with more understanding and knowledge. But the Lord will not continue to bless him if he is not obeying the principles that he already understands. If you want to increase your faith, you must analyze well the principles that you already understand and be sure to put those in order before you expect the Lord to provide you with much more. Because the Lord is merciful, he does not reveal to us great quantities of truth that might overwhelm us, because once we understand a principle, we become accountable for it.

President Brigham Young said something very interesting about faith:

> Belief and unbelief are independent in men, the same as other attributes. Men can acknowledge or reject, turn to the right or to the left, rise up or remain seated, you can say that the Lord and his Gospel are not worthy of notice, or you can bow to them. . . . Your own experience may satisfy you that faith is not brought into requisition by the presentation of either facts or falsehoods to the external senses, or to the inward perceptions of the mind.

In other words, neither facts nor falsehoods necessarily affect faith one way or another. Faith ultimately comes from within.

> If we speak of faith in the abstract, it is the power of God by which the worlds are and were made, and is a gift of God to those who believe and obey his commandments. On the other hand, no living, intelligent being, whether serving God or not, acts without belief. He might as well undertake to live without breathing as to live without the principle of belief. *But he must believe the truth, obey the truth, and practice the truth, to obtain the power of God called faith.* (*Discourses of Brigham Young*, compiled by John A. Widtsoe [Salt Lake City: Deseret Book Co., 1977], p. 153; italics added.)

If we are going to practice the truths we already know, we must be more careful to listen to the promptings of the Spirit. I am convinced that we receive many promptings for every one or two that we obey. We do not obey the promptings because we sometimes do not know that we are being prompted or because we think the promptings are from some other source within ourselves. I have learned in my limited experience that as we grow and become more spiritually mature, we will find that there are more and more promptings to help guide us to perform according to that which we already know.

Keeping the Commandments

In a way, keeping the commandments is the same as living by what we already understand. But it includes the idea that we are continuing to seek knowledge of *all* the commandments and to live by them. Joseph Smith wrote:

> The rights of the priesthood are inseparably connected with the powers of heaven, and . . . the powers of heaven cannot be controlled nor handled only upon the principles of righteousness. (D&C 121:36.)

Probably the greatest counsel that anybody could give you, if you want to increase your faith, is that faith will come according to your personal righteousness. I stress the word *personal* because sometimes people feel that they can be exalted because of a good mate or a good family. But the truth is that each person must be personally worthy.

There is a powerful connection between worthiness and faith. John the Beloved explained it this way:

> Let us not love in word, neither in tongue; but in deed and in truth.
>
> And hereby *we know that we are of the truth*, and shall *assure* our hearts before him.
>
> For *if our heart condemn us, God is greater than our heart, and knoweth all things*.
>
> Beloved, *if our heart condemn us not, then have we confidence toward God*.
>
> And *whatsoever we ask, we receive of him, because we keep his commandments*, and do those things that are pleasing in his sight. (1 John 3:18-22; italics added.)

This great apostle is teaching us that if we can pray with confidence that we are *trying* to be sinless, not that we are perfect, but that we are trying to live up to what we know to be right, then we will have the assurance that what we ask for, the Lord will grant. If, on the other hand, our hearts condemn us, it will be very hard for us to muster up the confidence to ask the Lord for a blessing. When our own hearts condemn us, we cannot obtain the faith and assurance necessary. Do you feel that your heart is right before God? I hope and pray that it is, and that if it is not, you are trying to make it so.

Sacrificing through Trials and Tribulations

You may greatly increase your faith through sacrifices, trials, and tribulations. The Lord has said:

> Verily I say unto you, all among them who know their hearts are honest, and are broken, and their spirits contrite, *and are willing to observe their covenants by sacrifice—yea, every sacrifice which I, the Lord, shall command—they are accepted of me.* (D&C 97:8; italics added.)

It is rather easy to make a covenant. As members of the Church we make many covenants. But the Lord is asking for more than that. To make the covenant is only the beginning. Then we must keep the covenant by sacrifice. In other words, the Lord is going to prove us to see if by sacrifice we will keep the covenants we have made. I am convinced that we must place on the altar of the Lord a spiritual sacrifice that is acceptable to him.

You need to look closely at your own life for the things that the Lord wants you to sacrifice. Most often, he wants us to give up our sins. He requires the sacrifice of a broken heart and a contrite spirit. (See 3 Nephi 9:20.) And when you do sacrifice what the Lord requires, you will see your faith increase.

The *Lectures on Faith* note:

> A religion that does not require the sacrifice of all things never has power sufficient to produce the faith necessary unto life and salvation; for, from the first existence of man, the faith necessary unto the enjoyment of life and salvation never could be obtained without the sacrifice of all earthly things.

You must be willing to sacrifice all earthly things. This does not mean that the Lord will *require* you to do it, but that you must be *willing* to do it. You must be willing to sacrifice whatever the Lord requires, even your own life, if necessary. If you are willing to do that, then you can lay claim to this great gift of faith. *The Lectures on Faith* continue:

> It was through this sacrifice, and this only, that God has ordained that men should enjoy eternal life; and it is through the medium of the sacrifice of all earthly things that men do actually know that they are doing the things that are well pleasing in the sight of God. When a man has offered in sacrifice all that he has for the truth's sake, not even withholding his life, and believing before God that he has been called to make this sacrifice because he seeks to do his will, he does know, most assuredly, that God does and will accept his sacrifice and offering, and that he has not, nor will not seek his face in vain. Under these circumstances, then, he can obtain the faith necessary for him to lay hold on eternal life.
>
> It was in offering sacrifices that Abel, the first martyr, obtained knowledge that he was accepted of God. And from the days of righteous Abel to the present time, the knowledge that men have that they are accepted in the sight of God is obtained by offering sacrifice. And in the last days, before the Lord comes, he is to gather together his saints who have made a covenant with him by sacrifice.
>
> Those, then, who make the sacrifice, will have the testimony that their course is pleasing in the sight of God; and those who have this testimony will have faith to lay hold on eternal life, and will be enabled, through faith, to endure unto the end, and receive the crown that is laid up for them that love the appearing of our Lord Jesus Christ. (*Lectures on Faith* 6:7, 9-10.)

The Lord told the Nephites the sacrifice that he requires:

> Ye shall offer up unto me no more the shedding of blood; yea, your sacrifices and your burnt offerings shall be done away, for I will accept none of your sacrifices and your burnt offerings.
>
> And *ye shall offer for a sacrifice unto me a broken heart and a contrite spirit.* And whoso cometh unto me with a broken heart

and a contrite spirit, him will I baptize with fire and with the Holy Ghost. (3 Nephi 9:19-20; italics added.)

I bear witness that faith is power. It is a spiritual power that transcends all that we can possibly imagine—it is the very power by which God operates. It is a power that will come over time, with patience and tribulation and much suffering. But it will come to the faithful who desire it and seek after it.

My prayer is that each of us will continue our search, probably an eternal search, to have more faith and to be more like our Heavenly Father and his Son Jesus Christ; and to worship them by the power of the Holy Ghost in all we do.

Questions to Ponder

1. Why did the district presidents and the Church members in the mission respond in faith so that they were able to raise the temple funds?

_____

_____

_____

2. Why were the mission counselors so full of faith?

_____

_____

_____

3. What six ways to increase faith are discussed in this chapter?

_____

_____

_____

4. Which of these things are you willing to begin doing today?

_____

_____

_____

5. How will you do them?

_____

_____

_____

6. As you read this chapter, you may have felt the promptings of the Spirit at certain places. Where were those places? What specifically was the Spirit prompting you to do? Will you do those things?

_____

_____

_____

Chapter Seven

Exercising Faith

A year or two after my mission, I gave a talk in a sacrament meeting in a ward other than my own. I had always thought that I was a relatively good speaker—have you ever thought that about yourself? It depends on who is gauging it. When I finished that talk, a good friend of mine, an older man full of wisdom, came up to me and said, "Brother Cook, why don't you believe in speaking by the Spirit?" He shook my whole image of myself as a speaker! I said, "What do you mean when you say that I don't believe in speaking by the Spirit?" And then he read me a passage from the Doctrine and Covenants:

> Neither take ye thought beforehand what ye shall say; but treasure up in your minds continually the words of life, and it shall be given you in the very hour that portion that shall be meted unto every man. (D&C 84:85.)

Then this good man said, "Now Brother Cook, I noticed that you developed an outline for your talk. You knew what you would talk about first and what story you would use to illustrate it, and so on. The Spirit may have wanted you to say something else but may have had a hard time getting through to you because you had already made up your mind about what you were going to say." Those words really burned. Then I thought, "But don't the general authorities read their talks in conference?" They do it so the translators can better follow what they are saying. I began thinking seriously about that after this man left. He was a great teacher because he left me with a great restlessness. Was he right? Did he really want me to walk up to the podium without notes or an outline? That was a big challenge to me. Searching in the scriptures, I found these words:

> Therefore, verily I say unto you, lift up your voices unto this people; speak the thoughts that I shall put into your hearts, and you shall not be confounded before men.

What a great promise! "If you speak *my* words you will never be confounded before men." Then he says:

> For it shall be given you in the very hour, yea, in the very moment, what ye shall say.

He is saying that he will give you at the very moment what he wants the listeners to know—how exciting that is! Now here are some conditions:

> But a commandment I give unto you, that ye shall declare whatsoever thing ye declare in my name, in solemnity of heart, in the spirit of meekness, in all things.

Then he gives a promise:

> And I give unto you this promise, that inasmuch as ye do this the Holy Ghost shall be shed forth in bearing record unto all things whatsoever ye shall say. (D&C 100:5-8.)

I began to realize that instead of having thought out what I might say, that I should give the Lord a chance to put thoughts into my mind, and that I should exercise the faith that he would tell me what I should say. About two weeks after that experience with my friend, the bishop of my own ward came up to me and said, "Brother Cook, we would like to have you give a talk in sacrament meeting." I remember the sick feeling that crept into my heart, but I said that I would do it.

As he walked away, I said to myself, "Oh, no! Here is the challenge to see what your faith is made of." I thought, "Well, my dad and mom think that I'm the best speaker in the world. If I just get up there and ad lib for twenty minutes, what will they think?" We always kidded in our family about who was the best speaker among my brothers. We had a kind of tradition going that probably had grown into something that it shouldn't have in trying to give a talk—for the right reasons, I hope. But I was concerned about trying to impress Mom and Dad and all of my family. Then I thought, "The bishop thinks I am a pretty good fellow. What if I stand up there and nothing comes out?" All those doubts began to creep in.

Unfortunately, that's where I was in my faith in those days, and you have to start progressing from where you are. I worried and prayed about what I was going to do. I thought that perhaps I would outline a talk and then leave the outline at home so that I would have a rough idea of what to say. I tried to select a topic, but I could not do it. I wrestled with one idea and then with another and I just could not feel good about any of them. The days kept clicking off until it got down to the day before, and I still couldn't settle on anything. I then descended to the lowest point in my faith during that experience when I finally said in my heart, "All right, I am going to get up there and try it, but just in case, I will have a spare talk in my pocket!" And then I heard the Spirit say, "Brother Cook, do you believe or do you not? It is that simple." I had to say in my heart, "Yes, I believe."

So I didn't plan anything for my talk. I just read the scriptures. It was all I could do to keep from thinking during the sacrament, "Now listen, you crazy guy, you have got to settle on something. At least think of a topic and a few ideas—a couple of stories or something. You have only five more minutes and you are on!" It took tremendous discipline not to do it. I will never forget walking up to that podium, knowing that my mind was empty. I was really exercising my faith, and I prayed, "Heavenly Father, if you don't come through on this one I am done!" *I really prayed with all of my heart.*

Then as I stood up there I felt something come over me that

just carried me away, and I spoke by the Spirit of the Lord. To this day, I do not know what that talk was about, but it was a great spiritual witness to me that the Lord will work with us if we let him. I felt good about that talk because I felt that the Lord had given me what to say, and after the talk a number of people were moved to repent by the Spirit, who worked through me in that instance. Several people said, "Brother Cook, what happened to you? I felt something that has caused me literally to change. I will never be the same." It was a great witness to me that if we exercise our faith in the Lord, he will honor his words. He has said:

> I, the Lord, am bound when ye do what I say; but when ye do
> not what I say, ye have no promise. (D&C 82:10.)

If we have faith in the Lord, how do we exercise that faith to bring about his eternal purposes? There are many factors involved.

Faith Is Exercised through Words

At times I have gone with other brethren to give a blessing to a person, and someone will say, "Now, brethren, let's exercise our faith," and some of the brethren will clench their fists and tense their muscles as if somehow, by doing that, they could exercise their faith. But exercising faith is a spiritual process, not a physical one, and it includes the use of words.

The *Lectures on Faith* say:

> What are we to understand by a man's working by faith?. . .
> We understand that when a man works by faith he works by mental exertion instead of physical force. *It is by words, instead of exerting his physical powers*, with which every being works when he works by faith. God said, "Let there be light," and there was light. Joshua spake, and the great lights which God had created stood still. Elijah commanded and the heavens were stayed for the space of three years and six months, so that it did not rain: he again commanded and the heavens gave forth rain. All this was done by faith. And the Savior says, "If you have faith as a grain of mustard seed, say to this mountain, 'Remove,' and it will remove; or say to that sycamine tree, 'Be ye plucked up, and planted in the

86

midst of the sea,' and it shall obey you." *Faith, then, works by words;* and with these its mightiest works have been, and will be, performed. (*Lectures on Faith* 7:3; italics added.)

There are scores of passages that indicate that faith is wrought not by physical exertion, but by words. The Book of Mormon prophet Jacob said:

> Behold, great and marvelous are the works of the Lord. How unsearchable are the depths of the mysteries of him; and it is impossible that man should find out all his ways. And no man knoweth of his ways save it be revealed unto him; wherefore, brethren, despise not the revelations of God.
>
> For behold, *by the power of his word* man came upon the face of the earth, which earth was created *by the power of his word.* (Jacob 4:8-9; italics added.)

In the scriptures, when *word* is capitalized, it means Jesus Christ. Here, however, it means the actual word that came out of the Lord's mouth.

Now consider these passages that teach that faith is exercised by words:

> And so great was the faith of Enoch, that he led the people of God, and their enemies came to battle against them; and *he spake the word of the Lord*, and the earth trembled, and the mountains fled, even according to his command; and the rivers of water were turned out of their course, and the roar of the lions was heard out of the wilderness; and all nations feared greatly, *so powerful was the word of Enoch, and so great was the power of the language which God had given him.* (Moses 7:13; italics added.)

> For the brother of Jared *said* unto the mountain Zerin, Remove—and it was removed. And if he had not had faith it would not have moved; wherefore thou workest after men have faith.
>
> For thus didst thou manifest thyself unto thy disciples; for after they had faith, and did *speak in thy name*, thou didst show thyself unto them in great power. (Ether 12:30-31; italics added.)

> But remember that all my judgments are not given unto men; and *as the words have gone forth out of my mouth* even so shall they be fulfilled, that the first shall be last, and that the last shall be

first in all things whatsoever I have created *by the word of my power, which is the power of my Spirit.*

For by the *power of my Spirit* created I them; yea, all things both spiritual and temporal— (D&C 29:30-31; italics added.)

And whatsoever they shall speak when moved upon by the Holy Ghost shall be scripture, shall be the will of the Lord, shall be the mind of the Lord, shall be *the word of the Lord*, shall be the voice of the Lord, and *the power of God* unto salvation. (D&C 68:4; italics added.)

Sometimes as I have watched missionaries, members, or others attempt to exercise their faith, the words of Joseph Smith ring in my mind that one means of exercising faith is through words.

You Must Be Personally Worthy

The Prophet Joseph Smith taught, "Faith is the foundation of all righteousness. You will not attain anything from the Lord lest you are keeping the commandments and to the degree that you are keeping the commandments is the degree that you will collect the blessings." I was impressed as I watched Harold B. Lee when he became the president of the Church. Many reporters gathered around him at that first press conference in Salt Lake City and said, "President Lee, what great counsel do you have for the Latter-day Saints?" Most of them probably thought that he was going to come out with some new policy or doctrine, but all he said was, "Yes, I do have some counsel for the Latter-day Saints. I tell them just one thing—Keep the commandments." When President Spencer W. Kimball was called to be the president of the Church, he said the very same thing. And Adam and Eve, and Moses, and all of the other servants of the Lord have said the same thing. The whole book of Deuteronomy seems to have one central message—Keep the commandments. How simple those three words are! And they are the foundation of exercising faith. You will not collect any blessing from the Lord short of your own individual personal righteousness.

We talk a lot about authority and power in the priesthood,

and there is both. It is reasonably easy to give someone the authority—put your hands on his head and confer it. But the power is a different issue. The power of the priesthood depends on your own righteousness. The Lord said:

> Behold, there are many called, but few are chosen.

And why are they not chosen?

> Because their hearts . . .

He didn't say their minds, he didn't say their attention—he said their hearts—circumscribing everything.

> . . . are set so much upon the things of this world, and aspire to the honors of men, that they do not learn this one lesson—

I don't know anywhere else in the scriptures where the Lord says "this one lesson." It must be very important. Now here is the lesson:

> That the rights of the priesthood are inseparably connected with the powers of heaven, and that the powers of heaven cannot be controlled nor handled only upon the principles of righteousness. (D&C 121:34-36.)

If you want to learn to exercise your faith, you must start with yourself—you must be in order. The Lord doesn't require us to get into order all at once or no one would ever get anywhere. We get into order a little bit at a time as we go along and as our understanding expands. As we become wiser and learn more from the scriptures and from the Lord, then we are more capable of getting into order. We begin to learn that more things aren't right; we repent; the Holy Ghost is able to be with us in more abundance and to teach us more; and our faith increases. Finally we reach the point where our sins are sins of omission instead of commission, and the process goes on.

The Power of Faith Is Spiritual and Is within You

Faith is spiritual; it comes from the Lord. But it is actuated by you. Suppose you know someone you want the Lord to help (an investigator or a wayward son, for example). What we sometimes tend to do is say, "Father in heaven, please bless Brother————. He is my home teaching companion and he is having difficulty with his testimony. Please send thy Spirit and change his heart." Often the Lord does answer such prayers, but it often takes a greater exertion of our faith to cause some righteous thing to occur.

Alma and the other Church members prayed for the Lord to turn the heart of Alma the Younger. They had sufficient faith that they literally *brought* an angel out of heaven.

When the Brother of Jared saw the Lord, was it because the Lord said, "Well, he is a pretty good man. I guess I will just show myself to him"? No, the brother of Jared learned a law and obeyed it. Note these words from the book of Ether:

> And the Lord said unto him: Believest thou the words which I shall speak?
>
> And he answered: Yea, Lord, I know that thou speakest the truth, for thou art a God of truth, and canst not lie.
>
> And when he had said these words, behold, the Lord showed himself unto him, and said: Because thou knowest these things ye are redeemed from the fall; therefore ye are brought back into my presence; therefore I show myself unto you.
>
> And because of the knowledge of this man he could not be kept from beholding within the veil; and he saw the finger of Jesus, which, when he saw, he fell with fear; for he knew that it was the finger of the Lord; and he had faith no longer for he knew, nothing doubting.
>
> Wherefore, having this perfect knowledge of God, he could not be kept from within the veil; therefore he saw Jesus; and he did minister unto him. (Ether 3:11-20.)

The Lord acts on his own, of course, but often he chooses to act according to our faith. The Lord says in a number of places, "I dwell in you and you in me." The Spirit of the Lord is in you. The Spirit of Christ is in every living thing. I think often the Lord says, "Don't ask me to do it—you do it." Satan would like to have it the other way. If you were dependent on the Lord to do all of the work, which is what Satan wanted and still wants, you would be a puppet on a string. But because of the great love of the Lord, he says, "I will give you some of my power until you learn to act independently, just as I do, if you will do my will. And if you will, I will eventually give you all my power."

I am convinced that Alma understood this idea thoroughly. He says in Alma 29:

> I ought not to harrow up in my desires, the firm decree of a just God, for I know that *he granteth unto men according to their desire*, whether it be unto death or unto life; yea, I know that *he allotteth unto men according to their wills*, whether they be unto salvation or unto destruction. (Alma 29:4; italics added.)

Alma doesn't say that God grants to us according to the circumstances, such as whether it is hot or cold, whether people help us or don't help us, or whether the time is right. He grants to us according to our wills. In other words, *it is up to you.*

The burden is there where it belongs. Elder James E. Talmage said, "Somehow the Latter-day Saints have the mistaken notion that in the end, when the day comes that the Lord will make them gods or goddesses, when someone lays their hands on their heads and, as it were, says to them, You have now all that you need to be a God—go ahead—this is not true. All that you need to be a God is in you right now. Your job is to take those crude elements within you and refine them."

When I was a mission president, occasionally a missionary would come up to me and say, "Elder Cook, I am going home. I can't do this—it is too hard." Would he have thought that he couldn't do it if he had known full well who he is? He was wasting his time talking to me—I wouldn't have believed it in a million years. The power is in us to bring to pass the Lord's will. The Lord has said:

> For behold, it is not meet that I should command in all things; for he that is compelled in all things, the same is a slothful and not a wise servant; wherefore he receiveth no reward.

In other words, the Lord is saying, "Take the reins. Take

charge under the direction of my Spirit. Don't wait for someone to tell you everything to do."

> Verily I say, men should be anxiously engaged in a good cause, and do many things of their own free will, and bring to pass much righteousness;
>
> For *the power is in them*, wherein they are agents unto themselves. And inasmuch as men do good they shall in nowise lose their reward. (D&C 58:26-28; italics added.)

Orson Pratt said this:

> [The mind] is the agent of the Almighty, clothed with mortal tabernacles and we must learn to discipline it, bring it to bear on one point and not allow the Devil to interfere or confuse it nor divert it from the great object that we have in view.
>
> If a person trains his mind to walk in the Spirit and brings his whole mind to bear upon its operations and upon the principles of faith, which are calculated to put him in possession of the Power of God, how much greater will be his faculties for attaining knowledge.

To exercise our faith we must discipline our minds. Many people are still struggling with their bodies, and some of us who are older are struggling with our bodies so that they will do what we want them to do. I talk a lot to myself. I don't know if that is healthy or not, but I remember a professional counselor saying to me that creative people always talk to themselves, and that made me feel a little bit better! So I kept doing it. I have to say to my body, "Now listen, who is in charge here?" Because the real Gene Cook is a spirit entity, isn't he? I am in charge here, and this body is here as my tabernacle. When my body wants to do something that my mind does not, I ask, "Who is in charge here—you or I? I am. Now let's move!" And my body obeys. We can do the same thing with our minds. The Lord gave us power to make it be so. What I am saying is this: You prevail over people, things, and situations by your faith.

You Must Not Exercise Your Faith Contrary to the Lord's Will

Remember that faith is conditioned on the will of the Lord as well as the will of man. In other words, if I pray for someone with all of my faith, but it is against the will of the Lord, who is going to win? The Lord will. His will is going to prevail—not always in the short run, but in the long run. I am sure that his will is that all men repent—it says that in the scriptures—but they don't. I am sure that the will of the Lord was that Nephi obtain the plates. Nephi failed twice before he succeeded. At first he didn't specifically follow the will of the Lord in how to obtain the plates, although his persistence eventually took him to the final result of accomplishing the will of the Lord.

Give Your Whole Heart to the Lord

When you are exercising your faith in something, you have got to give your whole heart to it—you can't do it part way. The Lord will help you only to the extent that you are able to give your heart. If you can give a little bit today then he will respond to that. The more you learn to give it, the more you will feel his presence.

The Lord said, "Look unto me in every thought; doubt not, fear not." (D&C 6:36.) That is a very strong commandment. As we concentrate our whole soul on some righteous purpose, it will come about.

It is possible to measure your faith by the number of your predetermined righteous desires that are fulfilled. In other words, if I say that I am going to do something and then fulfill it, that is a good measure of my faith. Some people float through life without taking a stand. They never say, "This I will do," and mean it. They just say, "Whatever will be, will be."

Consider a mission president who says, "How many people are you going to baptize this month, Elder?"

And the elder says, "Well, I don't know; that all depends."

"Depends on what?"

"Well, you know the members aren't helping us too much around here."

"Well, what does it depend on?"

Then the elder says, "Well, it is too hot," as if his success depended on something other than himself and the Lord. You should commit yourself to something that causes you to exercise your faith with your whole soul.

Go beyond the Edge of the Light

To exercise faith, you have to go beyond the edge of the light—you have to risk something. I remember the story about the fellow who fell off a cliff and was hanging onto a bush over a four-hundred-foot drop-off. He started praying, "Lord save me, save me. This branch is ready to go. I have only another minute or two." The Lord appeared above him and said, "Let go, and I will catch you." That is what it's all about, isn't it? Faith precedes the miracle.

I remember a fellow who wrote a book about losing weight. He weighed about 220 pounds six months before the book was to be published. He wrote in that book, "I now weigh 147 pounds. I am delighted with this new weight." And then he gave a description of how he felt at 147 pounds, but when he wrote it he was still 220. Was he risking? He had to weigh 147 when the book came out in six months. And he did. Do you see how he conceived that beforehand and then made it come into being? You can decide what you want to have happen and then bring it to pass. Do you believe that? It is true.

If you just stay within the realms of what you can do on your own, you can't expect to accomplish much. Some people say as they sit by a stove, "Give me heat and I will give you wood." That's ridiculous, isn't it? You know you cannot get heat from a stove unless you give it wood. But in the spiritual world we tend to want to do that. We say, "Lord, let me earn more money, and then I can pay my tithing." But the Lord says, "Pay your tithing and then you will prosper." We are willing to do the will of the Lord, but sometimes we pray, "Show me thy will and then I will do it." The Lord says, "No, do it and in the process I will show you my will."

The Lord reveals his will many times in half-steps. He does that so that we will be pressed into exercising faith in order to receive the other half. Why? So that we can be independent, as he is. When we walk beyond the edge of the light, then the lights of revelation come on. But until *we walk* to the edge of the light and do all in our power to perform, the Lord will not give us more.

He may reveal his general purposes to us, but most of the time the specifics will not be revealed until we have done all we can, and then the inspired specifics will come.

Be Completely Specific in Enumerating Your Righteous Desires to the Lord

A few years ago, I had lunch with a mission president and a certain district president. I asked the district president, "How many full-time missionaries are you going to have called by the end of this year?" It was then August 1, so that meant in the next five months. He answered quickly, which showed me that he had already thought out his goal, and he said, "I am going to have five." I said, "Okay, now that's August—what are you going to do in the other five months?" He said, "No, Elder Cook, that is five missionaries in five months." He was looking back because in that district they had never had five missionaries out at the same time—ever! He thought that going from zero to five was really something. But he was dealing with someone who had had some other experience. So I said, "Well, five is okay, but that ought to be just this month."

I kidded him a little to try to get him to raise his goal; he had to set his own goal—we couldn't set it for him. Then the mission president said, "You know, President, you could probably call twenty in those five months, couldn't you?" The district president said, "Oh no, twenty missionaries?" And then he started giving all the reasons why that was impossible. I asked him how many branches he had in the city and he said there were four. I asked him, "Well, could you get one missionary per branch per month?" He said, "Yes, I could do that—just one missionary per branch."

Do you see what he committed to? Twenty! Then I said to him, "President, I promise you that according to your faith and the faith of your leaders you will have twenty full-time missionaries called by December 31 of this year." The district met that goal— the following month alone they called ten full-time missionaries. To achieve a goal, you must know what it is—you must be specific. And it helps greatly to minimize that goal if you are very specific about it. If you talk about baptizing twenty people a month, it seems impossible, but if you talk about fewer than one a day, you can do that—you are talking about four families of five people. Of course you can baptize four families. What you are doing is making your goal smaller in your mind so that you can handle it.

President Kimball doesn't allow you to be with him without getting a commitment from you. He will be at a stake conference and say to the stake president, "What are you going to do with your Aaronic Priesthood during the next three months?" "Well, I don't know—it depends." "On what?" "I don't know." And then President Kimball says, "Why don't you select two or three goals?" And if the man can do it right then, he will, and if not President Kimball says, "We will be ending the conference tomorrow, and I will be meeting with you about noon. You be ready with your commitments and what you are going to do. I want to know specifically what they are and when you will have them fulfilled, and then I want you to tell me about it afterward." He is very specific because he loves people enough to help them grow.

Try to Be Completely Self-Disciplined

President David O. McKay said, "The first and best victory is to conquer self. To be conquered by self, is of all things, the most shameful and vile. One secret act of self-denial, one sacrifice of inclination to do is worth all of the good thoughts, warm feelings, and passionate prayers in which idle men indulge themselves."

When you say you are going to do something, then you do it. Keep your word. Don't be disappointed sometimes when you set a goal, but fail to attain it, for you can't know all of the time what the Lord's will is. Just exercise your faith in the Lord and do the best you can as to what you think his will may be. I often ask myself, "How much is your word worth, Elder Cook? What price could you put on your word? If you tell someone that you are going to do something, do you do it, or do you come up with excuses of why you didn't do it?" The Lord said:

> If a man vow a vow unto the Lord, or swear an oath to bind his soul with a bond; he shall not break his word, he shall do according to all that proceedeth out of his mouth. (Numbers 30:2.)

The Lord says in many places, "What I have spoken I have spoken, and I excuse not myself. Heaven and earth may pass away, but my words will not." In other words, what the Lord says will happen *will* happen. We are trying to acquire the Lord's attributes, aren't we? We want to be like him. One thing that will help us do this is to discipline our actions to fit our words. If your faith is weak, then in the beginning pick some smaller goals that you can discipline yourself to reach. They should be beyond what you feel you are presently capable of, but not too far.

We read in Ecclesiastes:

> When thou vowest a vow unto God, defer not to pay it; for he hath no pleasure in fools; pay that which thou hast vowed.
> Better is it that thou shouldest not vow, than that thou shouldest vow and not pay. (Ecclesiastes 5:4-5.)

It destroys my character, in my judgment, if I promise to do something and then I don't keep my promise when I could have. The thing you really want to promise is that you will do all in your power to accomplish the Lord's will—not necessarily a specific result. The result is up to the Lord. But how we discipline ourselves is up to us.

Be Willing to Offer Sacrifices

The Lord said:

> Verily I say unto you, all among them who know their hearts are honest, and are broken, and their spirits contrite, and are will-

ing to observe their covenants by sacrifice—yea, every sacrifice which I, the Lord, shall command—they are accepted of me. (D&C 97:8.)

In other words, it is rather easy to make a vow or a promise, but where it is going to cost you is where you sacrifice what is necessary to prove your faith by your works. The Lord wants us to prove to him by our sacrifice that we really believe—that we will do what is in our power to do to bring about his will.

There is one caution about this, however. I don't know how to say it any better than that some people spiritually get into a cactus garden, as it were, on this principle, knowing full well that they could get out of the garden if they would kick the right cactus. But there are about 356 cactuses in the garden, and they go around screaming until they have kicked them all. They kick against the pricks, as it were, feeling that they are doing all in their power to do their part—but they are overdoing it and not allowing the Lord to come in and do his part. They might have kicked ten cactuses and have hurt enough, and the Lord would have said, "Okay, that is enough," and would have allowed them to walk out. But some people are of the nature that they are going to kick them all. If they want to do that, the Lord will let them. But the unfortunate thing about it is that they are wasting a lot of time when they could have gone beyond that principle and been on to another one. The Lord will let you learn lots of things by your own experience, but sometimes you can be delivered a lot quicker if you let him deliver you. Moses could have said, "The way to get through this Red Sea is to get a lot of buckets." But he didn't say that—he just did all that he could reasonably do within his power, and then the Lord manifested his arm and accomplished a great miracle.

Be Aware of, and Use, Spiritual Evidences to Build Your Faith

Learn to watch for and recognize the spiritual evidences that come from exercising faith, for when you see them, your faith will grow. Also, as your spiritual awareness increases, so will the spiritual evidences that you will notice. And these, in turn, will increase your faith even more. Then you will receive more evidences, and eventually you will have a perfect knowledge that the Lord lives and that he rewards those who seek him in faith.

Use Apparent Failures to Strengthen Your Faith

In the face of apparent failure, double your faith, remembering that the Lord's will ultimately will prevail.

When we were to have our last baby in Uruguay, Sister Cook was the biggest that she had ever been. Usually she gains about twenty pounds or so with her pregnancy, but this time she gained forty-two pounds—she was big! In Uruguay they don't believe in having babies with saddle-blocks or shots. They believe in natural childbirth. Sister Cook had never had a baby that way. She had a rough last couple of months when she realized how big she was, and the doctor kept telling her that it would be the biggest baby she had ever had. She did all she could to prepare for the delivery by exercises and other techniques. When we reached the date that the baby was due and then passed it by a week, the doctor said on Friday, "Mrs. Cook, if the baby doesn't come by Monday we will have to induce labor, because the baby is too big."

Sister Cook and I went home and decided that we would exercise all our faith that the Lord would bring the baby naturally, because we didn't want it to be induced. We wanted the Lord to bring the baby in His own way. We prayed hard and fasted about it, and we went on some *long* walks!

That Sunday night—the day before we were going to go in—the baby still had not come. The next morning came and we went to the hospital at nine o'clock. I remember thinking, "Elder Cook, what is going to happen if the baby doesn't come naturally as a result of exercising your faith? What is your spirituality going to be like if this doesn't happen the way you are praying for it to happen?"

It is during such moments that you have got to commit to yourself and to the Lord, "I will not harden my heart and be angry if this thing doesn't come about. I will double my faith in the

Lord—not just that the incident will come about." About ten o'clock the nurse came in, and up until that very moment when they put the needle into my wife's arm, we believed that the baby would come naturally. But it didn't. Still, we felt good to know that right up until the very last second when they pierced her skin with the needle, we believed. When the baby came it was one of the greatest painless deliveries my wife has ever had. What a great spiritual experience it was.

I tell you that story to show you that things do not always work out in the way that you think they are going to. But what is important is what you do with your heart when things don't come about the way that you thought and planned. It is easy to believe when things are going well, but it is difficult to believe when they are not. But such trials are necessary to prove where your faith lies—is your faith in the Lord, or is it in what *you* want? The Lord will prove you to find out. Our attitude should be like that of Job, who, after losing all, said, "The Lord gave, and the Lord hath taken away; blessed be the name of the Lord." (Job 1:21.)

If you desire great faith, be prepared for great trials. They will come—I promise you they will. But we can use them to strengthen our faith in the Lord. The Apostle Paul said it beautifully:

> Therefore being justified by faith, we have peace with God through our Lord Jesus Christ:
>
> By whom also we have access by faith into this grace wherein we stand, and rejoice in hope of the glory of God.
>
> And not only so, but we glory in tribulations also; knowing that tribulation worketh patience;
>
> And patience experience; and experience hope.
>
> And hope maketh not ashamed; because the love of God is shed abroad in our hearts by the Holy Ghost which is given unto us. (Romans 5:1-5.)

Expect God to Perform According to Your Faith

After you have exercised your faith, you can expect God to keep his promises and to bring to pass his will. He did this with Adam, with Noah, with Abraham, with Nephi, and with all his servants throughout history, and he will do it with you. He will fulfill all his words, and he will grant you your righteous desires according to your faith.

After writing to the Hebrews about the faith of the ancient patriarchs, the Apostle Paul said:

> The time would fail me to tell of Gedeon, and of Barak, and of Samson, and of Jepthae; of David also, and Samuel, and of the prophets:
>
> Who through faith subdued kingdoms, wrought righteousness, obtained promises, stopped the mouths of lions,
>
> Quenched the violence of fire, escaped the edge of the sword, out of weakness were made strong, waxed valiant in fight, turned to flight the armies of the aliens. . . .
>
> Wherefore seeing we also are compassed about with so great a cloud of witnesses, let us lay aside every weight, and the sin which doth so easily beset us, and let us run with patience the race that is set before us,
>
> Looking unto Jesus, the author and finisher of our faith; who for the joy that was set before him endured the cross, despising the shame, and is set down at the right hand of the throne of God. . . .
>
> Now the God of peace, that brought again from the dead our Lord Jesus, that great shepherd of the sheep, through the blood of the everlasting covenant,
>
> Make you perfect in every good work to do his will, working in you that which is wellpleasing in his sight, through Jesus Christ; to whom be glory for ever and ever. Amen. (Hebrews 11:32-34; 12:1-2; 13:20-21.)

Questions to Ponder

1. How is faith exercised through words?

_____

_____

_____

2. What is the relationship of faith and personal worthiness?

_____

_____

_____

3. What role does the Lord play as we exercise faith? What role do we play?

_____

_____

_____

4. How can we measure our faith?

_____

_____

_____

5. How is self-discipline related to faith?

_____

_____

_____

6. How is sacrifice related to faith?

_____

_____

_____

7. How can you be more specific in praying about your goals and problems?

_____

_____

_____

8. How can you know the Lord's will as you exercise your faith at this time?

_____

_____

_____

9. What can you do today to help yourself give your whole heart to the Lord?

_____

_____

_____

10. How can you use an apparent failure in your own life to strengthen your faith?

_____

_____

_____

11. What do you need to do in your life at this time to go beyond the edge of the light in exercising your faith?

_____

_____

_____

Conclusion

In chapter 1, it was suggested that the purpose of this book was to help you to increase and exercise your faith to solve a specific problem or to reach a specific goal. It was also suggested that you might have success in doing this by pondering the questions at the ends of the chapters, by studying the scriptures, by discussing the principles of faith with others, and, most of all, by praying constantly for help in understanding and exercising faith. I hope that you have found success in following these suggestions, and that you will continue to press forward until you understand more fully the power of faith and are able to receive all the blessings that your Father in heaven has in store for you.

Faith can only be understood by the Spirit of the Lord. It does not come by way of men, although the Lord can use a man to teach you something about it. I hope that the principles described have helped you to learn, and, more importantly, to apply, the principles of faith. The way that you can learn best is through your own experience, by searching out the Lord and deciding that you want to increase your faith even until you can lay hold on eternal life, and by determining that you will pay any price to do it. It will be the adventure of your life, the adventure you were sent here to experience.

Many different headings were used in this book to try to describe faith. One could never remember them all when exercising his faith. So as a final summary to what has been taught, may I suggest six steps that you might easily remember and that may help you when you are trying to exercise faith:

1. Be believing, with your desires single to the glory of God.
2. Commit and discipline yourself totally in word and deed.
3. Do all in your power to fulfill your part.
4. Pray as if all depended on the Lord.
5. Prepare for constant and intense trials of your faith.
6. Expect the Lord to perform according to his holy will and your faith.

I admit before you and the Lord that I understand very little about what it means to have faith in the Lord Jesus Christ. But I bear testimony that it truly is the power by which Jehovah works, and that it is the power that you and every other person need to have, because through it you may exalt yourself and your family and all those around you. I pray that the Lord will bless you that you might remember the true principles in this book, and that they might stand out above the things that might not have been quite as clear as they could have been. I pray that you will continue to study and pray about what it means to live by the power of faith, and that in so doing, you may be able to obtain peace in this life and eternal life in the world to come. May the Lord bless you to that end, I pray in the name of Jesus Christ. Amen.

Index